GUIDEBOOK
for PERFECT BEINGS

ALSO BY B. J. WALL

Handbook for Perfect Beings

GUIDEBOOK
for PERFECT BEINGS

B.J. Wall

HAMPTON ROADS
PUBLISHING COMPANY, INC.

Cover design by Rosie Smith/Bartered Graphics
Cover photograph by Steve Wall © 2001

Hampton Roads Publishing Company, Inc.
1125 Stoney Ridge Road
Charlottesville, VA 22902

434-296-2772
fax: 434-296-5096
e-mail: hrpc@hrpub.com
www.hrpub.com

If you are unable to order this book from your local
bookseller, you may order directly from the publisher.
Call 1-800-766-8009, toll-free.
Library of Congress Catalog Card Number: 2001091194

ISBN 1-57174-243-3
10 9 8 7 6 5 4 3 2 1

Printed on acid-free paper in Canada

This book is dedicated to "The Group"—

Peggy, Debbie, Ursula,

Rita, Skeet, and especially

Patsy and Elaine

TABLE OF CONTENTS

CHAPTER 1

Introduction

All of the words in the *Handbook for Perfect Beings,* except for the first chapter and the epilogue, are the angels'. Group sessions teaching these Universal Laws were conducted each week with the same group of people for almost a year. All of these sessions were led by one of four angels, mostly Michael. They spoke through me. Each session was taped and transcribed so that the book would be their words, not mine. Over one thousand hours of tapes gave birth to the book. Since it's so difficult to describe God as he or she, I will use They or Them in this book as I did in the *Handbook.* In listening to the tapes while transcribing, I particularly noticed the continuing patience, overwhelming love, and specific information these angels shared with the group members.

I have approached this guidebook as if you and I were sitting down face to face having conversations concerning all of the Universal Laws. As I shared in the epilogue of the *Handbook for Perfect Beings,* it has taken fifty-one years of this life to pull these laws together. The beauty is that I've been testing them all along, and nothing in the daily life experience is wasted. Everything is a potential lesson.

But these laws will be of no use to you if you can't make sense out of them and be able to apply them to your every-day life. That's why I am using life experiences to illustrate how they are so much a part of our lives. As in the *Handbook,* most of the illustrations concentrate on finances and rela-tionships. I have focused on these two subjects because they have come up in just about every conversation I have had. They are the two most frequently asked questions in groups or seminars. So it would seem that they are the most difficult to comprehend and change.

Remember first that these laws are not to be viewed as rules in the traditional sense. You cannot break them. Try to view these laws as blueprints to the universe that define and describe our soul's inner workings. If you notice, they aren't saying that this is the only way "or else." Quite the contrary, you will learn a lot of great stuff about yourself you probably haven't heard before.

They are saying, first, that not only are you very power-ful, but you are also creating your life.

Second, you are creating in circles all the time.

Third, the circles come back to you; not as punishment, but simply as the Creator's way of gently tapping you on the shoulder and saying: "Did you notice this? Is this what you want to do? Is it helping you? Because I want you to use every-thing there is in the universe to assist you on this path called life." This cause and effect is meant to get your attention. You have an opportunity at this time to change it, release it, or just do the same thing again. You always have choices and there are no wrong choices, just as there are no wrong paths.

Fourth, there have to be opposites in us and around us for there to be a complete, perfect whole.

Fifth, there is no judgment to this, absolutely none. The Creator doesn't judge us. But if we aren't using these guidelines to our benefit, it *feels like* we are being punished.

Sixth, you have within you all the help you need to do this—mainly your own, personal angels.

Seventh, you are perfect at all times and you experience perfect moments in your life. It's just a matter of redefining what perfect is to you. There is no need to wait for a final reward.

The eighth one basically says it all. You really can't go wrong, because we will all reach "home" eventually. This releases you from the notion that there is this "one right path" that somehow we have to find. It also says that since you are different, how you do and see things will be different. So there can't be only one way to reach our destination; there can't be only one set of rules that is right. Instead, the truth is in each of us. That truth connects us. How could there be anything that separates us?

But most of us don't tend to use them in a productive way. We think "good" or "bad" things happen to us rather spontaneously. It's almost like an ant at a picnic. You try to avoid the huge foot of God stepping on you, but you really want to get to that ham sandwich. So it feels like we really don't have much control over our life. But we do, and that's the entire point of this guidebook. If you are willing to test these laws, then you can discover for yourself just how powerful you are. That isn't something I can give to you in a book. The goal of this book is just to make you aware of what you already have. I can give you $5,000, but I can't give you happiness. It has to be your personal experience.

The first thing we tend to lose in this process of discovery is our sense of humor and joy. With all the rules and the fear of punishment, life becomes too heavy to bear. These laws are meant to free you, not give you more rules to live with. You don't have to buy anything (except the book) and you don't have to search for anything; you already have it. Each law tells you something about yourself that is both reassuring and enlightening. It ends with a promise that you will get where you are going, so start enjoying the journey.

Try to view these as blueprints that define and describe our unique abilities. They simply give order to all the nuts and bolts of the universe. Or you might see God as the creator of the computer and its programs. These Universal Laws are the rules of each program. You are the user and get to create anything you want within their guidelines. The beauty is that we always have many options and just as many choices. They are there for you to test over and over again, only to prove to yourself what powers you possess. God already knows everything there is to know about you, so why should you have to prove anything to Them? You have an eternal connection to the Creator that you can't lose no matter what you say or do. This connection is through your spiritual DNA or your soul, since we all are part of Their creation. So what would God need to do to possibly prove anything to us?

Instead, this process is about discovery and our quest. This system of order called the Universal Laws is in place to assist us in discovering who we really are and what we are capable of. This discovery and connection that we all have with God, each other, and all of creation is our spirituality.

It's our very personal connection to God and has nothing to do with the religion we choose to agree with. Our religion can be *an expression of* our spirituality, but the two are not the same.

We are taught separation from the first second of birth. First we are separated from our mother during childbirth. Then we become separated from our parents as we grow. We are taught moral and spiritual separation by defining all parts of our very beings as good and bad. Then we become separated from other humans through cruelty, pain, and loss. Finally we are taught separation from our God, who resides somewhere in space, by religion. The goal of this book is to reunite all these parts through our connection with each other. God is not in space, but, instead, right with you all the time. God is in the air you breathe and the sun you feel on your face. The Creator is in every part of Its creation. The final goal is to reunite those parts in yourself that you see as divided into one whole perfect being.

CHAPTER 2

You Have the Ability to Create Your Life

There truly is no such thing as luck, either good or bad. You create your own life every minute of every day, either consciously or subconsciously. We each like to think we have some control over our lives, but to actually be in charge of creating every part of them? We only want to take credit for the good things that happen to us. How could we possibly be doing all this creating? You are doing this right now through the thoughts rolling around in your mind. You are also creating when you speak as well as act. Did you know that your mind has been given the gift of creating through your spiritual DNA? It knows only to create. Therefore, your true role is not one of a victim in life, but a powerful partner along with God.

Let's imagine for a moment that you were the Creator of

the entire universe and had just created Earth and the people on it. You were feeling pretty pleased with everything and enjoying the beauty of it all. But you realized that you needed to figure out a way to empower these human beings so they would be able to share control over their lives and be responsible for taking care of your Earth. How would you do it? Would there be a system based on merit? So if a person abided by your rules 50 percent of the time, they received 50 percent of this power? Would it be based on their looks, or their culture, or their families? Maybe it would be based on how often they worshiped you.

Since you loved all of them the same, it made sense to give everyone this ability in equal amounts. It also made sense to place this power in the mind, since that's the center of creativity. That probably would be the last place they would look for it, but how they used it was totally up to them.

To further help them learn how to use this beautiful creative power on their own, a system needed to be in place. You would create this system of order so that the conditions would be the same for everyone and everything. Consequently, everyone would be creating their lives all the time through their thoughts, words, and actions with some assistance from you.

How Do You Create? By Thoughts

Imagination used to be a big part of my life as a child. I would spend hours making the best mud pies and spend equal time trying to convince my younger brother to eat one. After watching the weekly episode of *Tarzan*, we would spend hours in Africa. We would be running through the woods behind our house and splashing through a small creek that was actually a drainage ditch for the neighborhood. To us it was Africa. Sometimes we would get the guys to be the natives chasing us and other times the girls would do the chasing. Either way, our imagination created this world and made it feel real. It seemed natural as a child to create whatever it was you wanted.

What happened to that imagination? I believe as we became adults it matured from active fantasies into an occasional daydream. We accepted what others told us was real or not and accepted the limitations of impossible or improbable. We pushed these dreams back into our child's mind and handed over our true power of creating to those around us.

Interestingly enough, we are willing to accept the fact that great inventors, leaders, philosophers, or those people who have influenced and shaped history had "creative thoughts." Most of these people did not accept the limitations of "can't" or "impossible." Where did Isaac Newton or Thomas Edison get their contributions to mankind? They were born through thoughts labeled as ideas. All they were doing was using their creative ability unrestricted. They refused to accept others' limitations and, instead, listened to their own inspiration.

We tend to distance ourselves from these brilliant people because we see ourselves as "ordinary" or incapable of such creations. You do have the ability to create with your thoughts and you can't stop it, but you can certainly understand it. This is very important to comprehend because if we don't understand what we're doing, our creative thoughts are randomly jumping everywhere or being scattered. We are still creating but it's in scattered pieces. Our life will feel like it's out of control and overwhelming. Two other situations can also affect your ability to create productively: being stuck or trapped, and constantly reacting to chaos around you.

Random Thoughts

Random thoughts are the constant chatter that continues in our head day after day. It may be mental notes, noticing other people, or trying to get your day organized. It could be the constant flow of tasks that worries you throughout the workday. It may be directed occasionally by your attention to something or someone, but usually it seems to have a life of its own. It seems to just jump from one thing to another. It's an effort to teach ourselves to focus any thoughts. Yet, when we are able to do this, we find that we do accomplish unbelievable feats. How does that happen? The key is a Universal Law to this creating that says that as your thoughts leave your head, they go out and return to you in a circle. What you ask for does happen; it just might not happen as you thought it would.

These random thoughts that take up a great deal of our time create chaos.

A good example would be a friend of mine who learned to drive in Atlanta, Georgia, and Washington, D.C. When she gets behind a wheel she is on a racetrack and competing with everyone behind the wheel. Even when we were trying to have a conversation on a recent trip, she would interrupt by calling other drivers unmentionable names. The whole time we were traveling in the car she was yelling at other drivers, trying to beat them by lane switching, or cursing. Interestingly enough, the more she did this, the more crazy drivers she attracted. They just seemed to jump right in front of the car. By the time we arrived at our destination, she was exhausted and I was a nervous wreck. Her attention had been scattered to the drivers who got in her way. Mine was distracted by my fears of not arriving in one piece. I try not to ride with her often.

Chaos

There are no coincidences in life, because we are creating it. That means even when life feels like it is totally in chaos, there is order. You just aren't seeing it. This order says that since you are creating your own life and you are doing it in circles, you can change the outcome. *You can sit in the very middle of this chaos and say, "I know everything is just fine."* That very statement itself calls recognition to that power of order. It's saying, "I know there is some order here and I choose to create understanding or answers or calm."

It's like looking at a hurricane. Most of us are aware of how a hurricane works. The outside is total destruction, yet the very center of the storm is total calm. In accepting that you are probably unconsciously responsible for the chaos, you can choose which part of the storm you want to focus on. By acknowledging that everything has a purpose and is fine, you are consciously focusing on the center of the storm, or the calm.

For most of us, that's hard to do. When everything seems to be falling apart around us, we tend to just react. We usually expect the very worst scenario. Placing blame or constantly reacting emotionally to those things around us just prolongs the process. By claiming there is order and choosing to create it, you get out of the emotions and into a more logical place, where you can get some answers to help. Think about it: when you are emotional do you use your best judgment or do you just react?

Many people thrive on daily craziness. I know people whose life seems to be in constant chaos. It's one thing after another. As a counselor I have worked with lots of people who came to their sessions each week with some major catastrophe in their life. I asked some clients after many such sessions, why they thought they had so much trouble in their lives. One reply was: "I've never known anything else. I know that if something good happens to me, the other shoe will drop and something bad happens. After a while it's not so difficult, because you get used to it."

Eventually you have to wonder what is going on. It's easy to say that God is punishing us or we are being tested in some unknown way. It's much harder to admit that we created the situation and are, therefore, responsible to change it. It's much easier to tell others and convince ourselves that we are the victims of an angry God, ruthless society, or deprived childhood. Yet, how else would we begin to understand this power we have over our lives?

Try to put the situation in perspective to be able to say, "Thank you," no matter what is going on. This focuses on the best outcome possible, no matter what things look like at the moment. By thinking and saying this, you are controlling what you want to see. You are consciously choosing to create calm out of chaos. If you are able to do this, the Universal Law states that it has to come to you. Of course, you can spend some time trying to visualize what outcome you want from the situation. (Remember, if you want harm to come to another person or persons, it comes back to you eventually.) It's always your choice how you want to use this ability.

Being Stuck/Trapped

As a counselor, I tend to get called when people feel they are so stuck in life they are desperate. They may be trapped in a relationship; it may be their job, finances, business, family members, or physical and emotional illness. To describe this feeling, I often use the example of a hamster running as hard as he can on a wheel in his cage. You feel like you are at a dead end with no options. Also, it feels like you are running as fast as you can and getting nowhere. Most people know what I'm talking about. These people keep finding themselves in the same place or with similar people or attracting similar situations that seem to have no answers or control.

I had one client who was quite beautiful but kept attracting abusive men into her life. She had come to me because she didn't understand why. The relationship would start out beautifully. They would convince her that they would take care of her and even worship her. But eventually she would feel trapped and try to be independent. Of course, the current partner would feel very betrayed and angry and would show it physically and emotionally. Then she would feel like she deserved the battering as punishment for rejecting their "love," as they called it. We spent months working together on what it was she was looking for. For there to be change, she had to concentrate on her beliefs and actions, not on the "good and bad" of the partner. When she would leave one abusive partner, she would have another "lover" within several weeks. She never accepted the fact that in order to be attracted to other types of men, she would have to change her belief in what she wanted and what she deserved to have. She just didn't want to be the one responsible for her life. The last time I saw her in domestic court, she had been beaten and was trying to get away from her latest love.

Remember, as you are thinking, you're creating. More often than not you just react to something around you. If you look behind that reaction, you will find a belief that acts like a magnet pulling to you everything you don't want. If you connect a thought or a belief to a strong emotion, it's like glue, it's hooked. This could apply to positive or negative emotions. You can take any situation that is keeping you stuck and look at the belief behind the emotions. Emotions are good; I'm not saying they aren't. But often we let the emotions keep us so stuck, that we spend all of our energy and attention constantly reacting to things, people, and situations around us. To get out of the trap you first have to get beyond the emotions and look at what's keeping you there.

Another example of being stuck would be when you are worrying or obsessing about something. *When you spend time worrying, remember you are actually investing a good bit of energy creating what you don't want.* The mind doesn't know that this is what you don't want to happen. It just knows the command to create whatever you tell it. Is that what you want? See yourself as that hamster running constantly and getting nowhere.

It's very much like being in a dark cave. When you continually have thoughts and emotions going out that are only focused on your misery, not your ability to control, it's no wonder you feel trapped. That's when you say: "I have no choices. I'm miserable. What's my purpose in living? Why does the same thing keep happening to me?" Interestingly enough, that's when humans allow themselves to search. When they are desperate or feel they have nothing to lose, then they usually are willing to take chances and look for changes. If they are in there long enough, they start to search for some way out of the cave, no matter the cost. Maybe they have to become willing to quit their job and look for another. Maybe they have to be willing to look at themselves and see why they are attracting the same hurtful people in relationships. Sometimes they decide to go ahead and end things, it's just too miserable. So this feeling of being stuck is a sure sign that you are at a crossroads in your life and just can't see what options you have in front of you. It's an opportunity to decide which direction you want to go.

To get out of being stuck, worried, or obsessed, you must first admit that you have the power to change the situation through your thoughts. On one side, it's difficult admitting to ourselves that we could be creating the circumstances. On the other side, it's very powerful to acknowledge that if you created it or allowed it to happen to begin with, then you certainly can create a way out. Try to visualize that you are controlling with every thought that leaves your head. To do this you will have to put your emotions aside. It's difficult to be emotional and logical at the same time. Tell yourself that you will place your emotions in a closet inside you for at least thirty minutes.

CHALLENGE:

Fill in the blank. I feel stuck or trapped about _____ in my life. I will acknowledge that I have the power to change this. I will list my options and know they are all possible. I will take small steps toward one of the options.

During this time, look at *all* your options. You always have choices. Usually I've found that people will eventually acknowledge they have choices, they just don't like them. Where do you want to go? What do you want to accomplish? Usually at the very middle of this process is a belief that is holding you back. As you are looking at choices, ask yourself what fear is keeping you from taking them. Do you believe that you won't be able to get a better job if you quit your current one?

Could it be that you couldn't possibly be entitled to a great relationship because you feel you aren't worthy of it?

Fear tends to paralyze. Yet desperation is another way to overcome the fear. If you are in the cave, hungry, cold, and afraid, you can get to the point that you will begin searching in the darkness for something, anything, to help guide you to safety. You will take chances that normally you wouldn't. Oftentimes we have other help. We have a strong intuition or gut feelings that tell us what to do. Fear has a tendency to shout a little louder, so often we don't hear or trust our intuition but choose, instead, to trust our fear. The fastest way out of the cave is to acknowledge that we created the cave in the first place. What do we want to do with it? Being stuck has a purpose of its own: to give you time to reevaluate where you are going. If we created the cave, then maybe we needed some quiet time to explore what we want to do or how to change the direction of our lives.

Focusing

When you are able to focus on something, you are literally building it right in front of your eyes. It's coming together a piece at a time. What usually stops you from achieving what you want is that you have kept in your mind a narrow idea of what it's supposed to be or when it's supposed to happen. Consequently, as you build this thing you begin to realize this isn't what you asked for, so you tear it down. Then you get upset when it didn't happen.

When you catch yourself thinking or saying words like "can't," "impossible," "should," or even "shouldn't," you are tearing down what you have built. You have this ability to create anything you want inside of you. You've just forgotten. You know how to do this. You've gotten tangled up in the language you've been raised with, which includes "should," "could," "bad," "good," "right," and "wrong," as if there is only one way. No. There is no "one way" to learn something. Each of us is so different; it makes sense that how we are going to learn is very different. Sometimes you do have to just jump out there. Sometimes you are pleasantly surprised and other times you get exactly what you expected. But to blame it on something or someone else is to say that they have more power than you do. The reality is that you are as much a creator of your world as God is. You create in equal amounts; it is a partnership.

Think about the last time you really wanted something. It could be a relationship, a new car, job advancement, or even something as simple as money to pay a bill. How long could you keep that thought? Oftentimes we tend to ask for it, then in the next breath admit to ourselves it probably won't happen or we don't really deserve it. We stop it as soon as we start to create it. Listen to people. Most of the time their desires or dreams are followed by words that totally discredit their ability to get it.

Even those who have strong beliefs that something can or will happen, often limit how it can get to them. I find that most people have very narrow ideas of how they can receive money. The most obvious choice is through their job or friends or relatives. Maybe, just maybe, they might have an outside chance of winning the lottery. That's it. Those are all the choices you have to receive money. You think you have to earn it, inherit it, win it, or sell something.

I remember my fortieth birthday very well because we were having some major financial problems. Steve and the kids took the loose change they had collected to buy some chicken for dinner. There were no presents, but they did manage to cut a sign out of newspapers saying, "Happy Birthday BJ." We ended up losing our house and car that spring and it was difficult to "see" any other way to get money to live on. We fervently prayed and visualized constantly, but unknowingly limited how the money should come. Fear was a part of our daily lives as bill collectors threatened and hounded us day and night. We were stuck in the mentality that believed money had to come through our work. We had to reach a point where our fear of losing the house or the car just wasn't important anymore. Once we gave up our fears and the old way of thinking, life started to turn around. It took six months to get out of that situation, but it happened when we expanded our minds to additional options.

But you get frustrated. Even that frustration has a place in the cycle of creating. If you get frustrated enough, you're going to be willing to look different places and different ways to build what it is you're wanting. Avoid the frustration and leave the door open. Instead of creating just one or two ways to receive something, build many ways for it to come to you.

You are either constantly building something or tearing it down. When you have a thought, belief, or goal that you've been really focusing on but it doesn't seem to be working—it really is working. It is building, but sometimes it has to get to a certain point for you to be able to see it. Let's say that you asked for $500 to pay doctor bills. Four weeks later no money has come so you say, "I didn't get my $500, it's been four weeks, and so it must not be going to happen." What you built is still there, even though your thoughts quit. It can still come to you, but it just might need to come through different directions than you thought it should.

Most of us would expect to see the whole amount come

from one place. Maybe five $100 bills would come floating out of the sky. So we wouldn't be expecting it to come in $50s or $100s from different places. But what if you managed to get $150 in overtime in your check? Or maybe someone paid you back the $40 they had borrowed? We seem to have trouble acknowledging this is what we asked for. It's as if we are each looking for some miracle to happen to prove there is a God and we are worthy of this miracle. Instead, what happens is you spend a good bit of time irritated at yourself or God, whoever is more convenient, because this didn't work. It helps if you can immediately see yourself either building something or tearing it down with these requests.

CHALLENGE:

Fill in the blank. I need _____. This could start with something small like a hug or a compliment or even $50. See it done, say it out loud, and then say, "Thank you," and leave it alone. Don't limit how or where it could come to you. Pay attention and see what happens.

What Results Are You Creating?

When we make a request of God, we aren't really testing the Creator; we are instead testing our own boundaries and limitations. This whole thing of living isn't about proving yourself to the Creator or the Creator proving anything to you. It's about you proving just how powerful you are to yourself.

Now that you know that you are creating your life, what

are you expecting life to be as you deal with these ideas and try to use them? Are you expecting your life to be worry free and have every request immediately materialize in front of you? Maybe there would be no physical pain and everything you did would be wildly successful.

If you have been taught that perfect is a place where everything is peaceful all the time and everyone has everything they could possibly want, you might be surprised. Let's go back to the original question, "Will the ability to create by focusing give me all the money I need, perfect health, big houses, or great relationships?" That usually is the first question I get when I'm talking about our ability to create. The initial reaction is, "If I can do all of this, why don't I already have everything I need and want?"

What happens when we pray to God to give us a miracle for something and it doesn't happen? My answer to both questions would be because you changed or stopped it from happening. Since we are cocreators with God in this whole play we call life, we get to change it, even subconsciously. So you're really in control. Often I hear people ask, "Why didn't I get this or that? What you told me wasn't true." The human mind wants to control. To do that, it starts to analyze how you could receive your request based on logic and past experiences. Those two things aren't all bad by themselves, but when you do not ask for help in getting past logic and experiences, you don't grow. Logic alone isn't going to do it. Logic questions most of the things you hear. It uses words like "can't," "shouldn't," "wouldn't," or "impossible." So I would say then, by itself, it's not helping you. Past experiences can be very confining, particularly if you keep looking at them as being the only way it can be done simply because that's how it's always been. It's back to being a hamster in one of those wheels, running just as hard as you can. The whole time you are thinking you're going to get ahead and not understanding why you don't.

So when you ask for things, understand truly that you are also asking yourself, because you are the creator of your world. You have some responsibility in this. You certainly get help from God and your own angels, but don't stop it from happening because of your own doubt. Don't ask for something and then if it doesn't happen in two days, stop it by thinking, "I just won't believe that," or "I don't deserve it." You are shutting the door in your own face and on your own fingers. You have no one to look at but yourself, because you're the one who opens the door. Instead look at what limitations you are holding on to that are stopping you from receiving what's yours. The whole universe wants to give you all the things you ask for. You stop it through your thoughts and beliefs.

Let's take the last thirty minutes or so. Think back to what was in your head and what you were creating. Were you frustrated over something? Were you worrying about a family member, a friend, or money? Whatever it was you were thinking about that whole thirty minutes is what you were creating. I'm not saying that you have to consciously monitor or filter every second. But I'm saying start to be aware of your power, this genetic DNA, this very thing you've inherited from your Creator, and use it to your advantage.

So let's take an example of finances or the lack thereof. That first time you thought, "I won't be able to pay my bills right now," fear set in, the circle went out and came back. You were building the lack of money. Then if you're worrying about it to the point that you're concentrating on this for a few minutes, hours, or days, you are almost guaranteeing that it will happen. Each time the thought goes out and comes back you are literally creating a stronger version of that thing you are seeing. Since you are spending more time on thoughts relating to the fear of no money, why should you be surprised then when it happens? You've taken this power and created it and it has to be.

CHALLENGE:

Fill in the blank. I want _____. This could be something big in your life like a new house or car. Know that the universe wants to give it to you. You can visualize what it could look like, but don't limit yourself.

In accepting and gradually understanding this principle, you can look to results that create more calm than chaos. Your life is definitely going to be better in that you will have more control and understanding about how you are creating. You will recognize what you are capable of doing. You will be able to feel more in command of those random thoughts and will get out of chaotic situations more quickly. So you will be using them more efficiently. I'm not promising that you will have lots of wealth and be surrounded by friends that always adore you.

What is going to happen is that you will be able to release old beliefs and fears that stop you from being the powerful person that you already are. Often we are told by well-meaning parents, teachers, family members, and friends what is bad and what is good. We are told what we should do, could do, and are supposed to do. You were given all those alternatives to perfection and you accepted them as yours. With all of those rules and all those layers of disappointments in ourselves, it's no wonder we can't accept the idea that we might already be perfect. Living is just the releasing of those layers to discover what's underneath, and you've got your whole life to do it.

As you shed those layers, you get to discover it's all been a play. Each lifetime we have been actors on a stage. We've all been wearing costumes that we thought were our bodies. It's not really us. We've been reading a script and interacting with basically the same people play after play. Each time you go out on stage, you hear yourself say the same things, and you question them. Finally, one day you start to realize that you can change the script if you want to. Of course, all the people on the stage with you will certainly react to you when you do this. You're probably going to make them uncomfortable as they have to change their scripts too.

So How Do We Change Our Thinking?

Quite a few years ago, I began meditating in an effort to better control my thoughts. I believed that meditating meant I was supposed to totally clear my mind of any thoughts. I was trying to create dead silence in my head. But try as hard as I could, I just couldn't do it. I could slow the thoughts down, but couldn't turn them completely off. After many unsuccessful attempts, I realized that meditating meant to be quiet and just listen to my angels talk to me. Or maybe it meant to be quiet and allow myself to feel the connection to the universe in peacefulness. Even those short attempts to control my thoughts were difficult. How is it possible to control most of our thoughts in order to change our life if changing just one is so tough?

How do you start changing what you are creating? The answer is, one step at a time and one thought at a time. The first step is to acknowledge that you have the ability to create through your thoughts, words, and actions and are constantly doing it. The second step is to start paying attention to what you are creating through your thoughts. If you already know that most of your thoughts are going to be random, then you might try to focus during a small part of the day.

Do you realize that when you're waking up in the morning, those first thoughts actually prepare your whole day for you? The creative circle starts with that very first thought. The second your eyes open and that very first thought jumps from your mind, you have already started. You literally begin all the creative circles for your day at that moment and end with the last one before you go into a deep sleep.

So all day you're producing these circles as you constantly interact with people and things. If you wake up and your first thought is focused on "What is it I dread today or what do I have to do today?" it starts you off with a circle that catches up by the end of the day. Maybe some days you are worried about certain things or trying to plan what you've got to do. Start to put what you want in that time slot. Don't leave it blank to just fill in with clutter. That's what happens when you worry constantly or just react to everyone around you. That's when you think that everyone is treating you unjustly. If you don't place that first thought there, your old ones will rush in and keep you in turmoil all day. Sometimes it feels like somebody's behind you, pushing the whole time. If you have to do this or you absolutely have to get a certain task done, you usually don't get to enjoy it.

There really isn't someone behind you pushing. It is meaningless chatter, filling the empty places in your mind. So when you first get up, see the circle starting. Focus on what you want from that day. It doesn't matter what day it is. It doesn't matter if you go to work or not. It's what do you want.

CHALLENGE:

Take the first thought of the morning, and see the day calm yet productive. Just spend a few moments on this, then check back that night and see what happened.

Go back to that first thought. Let's say you change it and you make whatever you want for that day. You take a couple of minutes to create the picture you want, then release it. See the day flowing by as everything fits together. Throughout the day, when something gets your attention, be aware of it and direct it where you want to go. See each person you interact with as a potential teacher for you. At the end of the day, what did you learn, and from whom? If you choose to direct harm to someone, remember it will come back much bigger than when it left you. If it's sent with a more positive attitude, it will come back a hundred times stronger than when it left you, because the circle would have been larger.

Another way to start controlling those thoughts first thing in the morning is to see your mind as a blank canvas. When you wake up, the first thought takes a brush and creates a whole background of color or whatever it is you want. It can be a black cloud or it can be a beautiful blue sky. Then you fill in that painting with other things you are thinking during the day. You are creating a picture of your day. In doing that, you are creating your life—one day at a time, one minute at a time, and one stroke at a time.

Many of us wake up creating or reminding ourselves of this list of things we have to do. There is nothing wrong with trying to organize yourself, but it took a long time for me to realize that I was a slave to my list. To feel better, I would call my list goals. But at the end of the day it didn't matter what

I called them, I would still rate myself based on whether or not I accomplished them. If you use the word "should" in your list, that very word in itself puts a pressure on you that you have to do it or else. To my amazement the world didn't fall apart when I didn't accomplish half the things on this list. I've found out that some things really weren't important and if they didn't get done, they really didn't need to be done anyway. Seems like the important things get done.

People who have to have lists need them for control. It's just so easy to put your whole life on little lists and think it gives you a sense of direction. What if at your death you look back to what you accomplished? OK, you went shopping and you picked up the groceries or you cooked meals. What did you accomplish? What do you want to look at? Each one of us will be standing there looking backward, all the way back, not to be judged but to understand.

Instead, at the end of the day look inside you to see where you are compared to where you were in the morning. What have you absorbed that day? What did you learn? Who did you touch? Who touched you? Take your memories of that day and examine them much like you were looking at pictures in a scrapbook. People get so occupied with their lists they forget there are others around them. They get so intent to finish that list they forget to connect with all those people around them and miss so much.

CHALLENGE:

Start to pay attention to those small spontaneous wishes that you make that just seem to pop up in your head from time to time. Then let them go. See how long it takes for you to get what you ask for.

Sometimes you have days that you feel you do not want to be with people. There are reasons for it. The universe is not set up on a system that has to work from 9 to 5 or work so many days a week. You will have your job, you will get your money, and if you think that you won't, then you've given away your power. But if you have a strong desire to rest or be alone or your body is sick, you need to take some time for yourself. It's important to listen to your body, because if you don't, it will eventually force you to rest because you will be sick.

Look at the creation around you, even the trees, the flowers, and the animals. They rest for long periods of time, sometimes months. Humans think if they have a few hours in a night, they're okay; they can keep going because they're tough. You're not machines. You're energy. That's different.

How to Change Being Stuck/Trapped

1) Get in a quiet place alone.

2) Move your emotions out of the way by putting them in a closet.

3) Ask yourself what would be the absolute best option and the worst option for you. Then list all the other possibilities in between. Pick out your first, second, and third choices.

4) Once you've looked over the list, try to create a first step to your first and second choices.

5) What could be stopping you from taking a first step toward these choices?

6) Attempt to take that first step and then release everything else.

7) See what happens and know that everything is working for you no matter what things look like.

As we said earlier, being stuck is simply being at a crossroads in your life. It's like standing where the road splits or goes four different ways. You don't know which way to go. The universe is trying to tell you that you have an opportunity to go different directions and try new and different things. For most people this isn't good news. Most people are very afraid of change. I know people who have had the same daily routine for the last twenty years, down to eating the same foods at meals. They are terrified of change and will live in complete misery to avoid it.

In that misery the universe is trying to get you to look at your options. Most people will say they have no options—hence the word "stuck" or "trapped" like an animal. You didn't get trapped overnight. It happened gradually until you realized this isn't what you want. Something lured you into the sandpit or the trap and that something is probably keeping you there. You have to first determine what it is in order to release it. It probably started out as a challenge or an opportunity and somehow became a rock around your neck. For example, a relationship could have started as a feeling of being connected with someone and ended up feeling like you were responsible for everything. Or maybe it started with someone wanting to protect and care for you and it became a prison. You might have started that new job with excitement and then found, after several months or years, it wasn't what you thought. Whatever it is, it is definitely time to let it go. It isn't helping you anymore.

More times than not, I have heard clients and friends argue with me that they couldn't possibly get out of the relationship because they don't want to hurt the other person even if the relationship was abusive. Or maybe they might be worried about what others would think of them if they made changes. You have to be willing to open up your mind to the possibility that you are helping everyone by changing yourself. They get to see someone up close try a different direction or path. That tells them that they can change too if they want. What keeps you stuck is not the different options in front of you but the potential results that you think will happen.

If you are not able to see any of your choices, start with a dream or an old idea of where you want to be. This is like opening a door that is stuck. To get it open, you at least have to pry open a crack. A dream or idea is a start. To get the door open even more, you need to look at all, and I mean all, of the possible solutions that come to your mind. These can be realistic or not, it doesn't matter. What you are doing is creating lots of different ways for your direction to come to you. Being open provides those channels and starts those circles of creating.

Decide which choices you want to focus on and put them down on a piece of paper and keep them somewhere close. Be willing to take some chances as different opportunities approach you. You get to do this in steps, but you have to get out of the mud first. You really don't have to obsess on these choices. Since there really are no "bad" or "wrong" choices, you have a total freedom to choose. Just know that you have started the creative process and the Universal Law states that it will come back to you in the same form it was sent. Usually something will happen fairly quickly to guide you in a direction. You may think that you have to give up something to get out of the mud—and you do. It tends to be that thing that lured you there and kept you stuck as well. Whatever it ends up being, you didn't need it anymore. Instead, you will replace it with something even better.

A close friend of mine had always wanted to go on a cruise, but never felt she had enough money to do it. She was delighted when several of her older friends asked her to accompany them on a five-day cruise as their guest. For weeks she prepared for the trip, thinking her lifelong dream had come true.

In her words she tells the story: "I knew the ladies had asked me to go because they were older and had health problems but I really wanted to go. One of the ladies had terminal cancer, one had diabetes, and another was in her late seventies. I stepped right in, trying to do everything for everybody, but the more I did the more I had to do. I arranged for the car rental and drove the group from Atlanta to Ft. Lauderdale. One lady had diabetes and asked me to take care of her insulin. I spent the entire trip making sure there was ice everywhere we went.

"The cruise turned out to be a promotional thing where you had to listen to a sales pitch everywhere you went. As if that wasn't enough, the cabins we were assigned to were positioned just above the engines. The constant roar and the heat from them basically eliminated the possibility of any sleep. The air conditioning was broken most of the trip and the lights would go on and off.

"The real scare came on our way home when the engines stopped working. The last night of our journey everything was quiet with no engines. Of course there was no air conditioning, either. By the next morning there was no electricity on the entire boat and black smoke was coming out of the smokestack.

"When we finally got back to port, we were over thirteen hours late. People were crammed everywhere as some were trying to get off the boat and some were boarding. I was trying to get the ladies off the boat, get the luggage, and get the rental car from the compound before the gates closed. I had thirty minutes and was supposed to be waiting in three lines at once. I assigned each person to a task and frantically went to get the car. I managed to get it at the last minute, got the luggage, and finally reached my breaking point. I just sat in the car alone and cried and cried. I shouted to God and anybody else listening that I didn't want to ever be responsible for everybody and everything—only me.

"I have always had a problem with responsibility. I was always the one trying to see that everyone was happy and things went smoothly. The lesson I needed to learn on this cruise was that I was not responsible for anyone else and can't make everyone happy."

She got what she asked for, which was a cruise, yet she felt trapped by her commitment to these friends. The harder she tried to make everyone happy, the worse things got. Consequently she stayed in the emotions until she had enough. At that point, she was ready to let go her belief that she not only had to be responsible for everyone else, but had to keep them happy as well. It was an excellent lesson on responsibility.

How to Change Chaos or a Crisis

1) Choose to focus on the calm by going somewhere quiet and get out of the emotions. Take several deep breaths.

2) Remember you are the creator of this chaos and you can change it. It has a purpose in your life.

3) Ask God or your helpers what would be the very best way to change this or let go of it. The answer will be the very next words you hear in your thoughts.

4) Be willing to take the first step and wait.

5) Allow the universe to help you by not limiting the direction help can come from.

6) When everything has calmed down ask yourself what the purpose was and what was the lesson of the whole experience.

7) Praise yourself for doing such a great job.

As we said earlier, chaos usually tends to sneak up on you without much warning. Usually it attacks quickly and we react just as quickly with emotions. So the very first thing to do when you catch your first breath is tell your emotions to get out of the way for a while. That's not particularly easy, but since you are the one who created the chaos in the first place, you can control your emotions. They will listen to you for a little while at least.

The second step is to go straight to the core of that hurricane and find the peace and calm in the middle. Claim that calm by stating, "Everything is fine regardless of what things look like." You might have to say that several times before you start to feel calmer. Once things have settled down, ask yourself, "What do I need to do to handle this in the best way possible?" You'll get an answer as either a thought or an intuitive feeling. Often we get to the point we just say: "That's it! I've had enough! I'm letting everything go; I give up." Maybe that's what the whole experience was for in the first place. It was to know when to let go of a situation or problem. The hard part is trusting what you hear.

After you have done these steps, allow things to play themselves out. Trust in the universe and try to see only calm even if emotions arise. Remember that whoever or whatever is causing you the chaos has no more power than you do. When the chaotic situation is resolved, take some quiet time with yourself and ask, "What was it all about and what did I need to learn from this?" It doesn't matter whether you created it or allowed yourself to be pulled into someone else's hurricane; the whole purpose was to learn something. So it makes sense to ask the last question.

Letting Go Once You've Created It

In this process of creating, we tend to want to control every step of the process by trying to figure out logically how whatever we've asked for is going to happen. We also tend to want to jump in and do something. Your mind can get preoccupied with the task. Yet, when we create something, it isn't necessary for us to try to control it every step of the way. You've created it and you know it's going to travel in a circle, so all you really have to do is see the end result you want. You just say, "It's going to happen and I'm going to get on with my life in other things." Do you think the Creator sits around watching you and controlling every step you take to ensure that humanity turns out a specific way? No.

In other words, things flow so much better when you're not trying to control them. We each are beautiful, knowledgeable beings. But your idea of what things are supposed to look like and what they're probably going to end up looking like are different. Did you ever see a picture of a hairstyle in a magazine and take it to your hairdresser? You probably hoped you would look just like that model when you were finished. The fact that the model has a different face and that it took a team of people hours to make him or her look beautiful doesn't go through your mind. You just know that hairstyle will make you look every bit as great as that model. The few times I actually received the haircut I was expecting, I still left the salon feeling like something didn't work.

So if you are over here working with every ounce you've got trying to force the situation to fit into your plans, you might miss out on other requests you've made. You will get what you want if you stay with it long enough. But you could have gotten it eventually anyway. The reality is if you can let go of that need to control it, it flows like a small stream and picks up everything it needs to happen. You do get your answers; you do get what you've asked for with a lot less effort.

My husband has always had an office in our home. He usually has had to use old desks or pieces of furniture we found at thrift stores. For years he would wishfully state that he would love to have nice office furniture that matched. But then the next statement would be "when we can afford it." Now the first mistake was limiting the time "when we can afford it," which for most folks means retirement. The second mistake was limiting how it could come. He thought he had to buy it from an expensive furniture store.

A year ago he made his usual statement about the office furniture but didn't limit it. He just left it, knowing it would come. Within three weeks he was at an auction of an office supply store and bid on a beautiful solid walnut desk and credenza. He was shocked when he found the original price tags inside the drawers. He had purchased $12,000 worth of furniture for $145. A miracle? No, just creation in the process without the limitations or controls. The difference was he didn't say "when I can afford it." He left it alone, knowing it would happen.

Words and Actions

The reason I have spent so much time on thoughts instead of words and actions is because thoughts are at the very center of the creating process. Words and/or actions tend to follow. Whatever direction your thoughts are going, your words and actions usually follow. This doesn't mean that your words don't have power; they most certainly do. But they have to be directed by your thoughts first. Even if you don't always say exactly what's on your mind, you tend to soften it or change some version of it. I would go even further to say that the word is directed by the thought even when we say the opposite of what we are thinking.

I hear a lot of truth coming out of people's mouths that they try to disguise, saying "I was just kidding." No they weren't; they meant at least some of it. Oftentimes we say things that seem to slip out in spite of what we meant. But the truth is there is a thought or a belief behind what is said.

Whether it's thoughts, words, or actions, remember you are creating it. It doesn't matter if you meant to or not. It doesn't matter if you understand this or not—it's your creation.

CHAPTER 3

You Create in Circles

Most of my adult life I have heard the cliché "Be careful what you ask for because you might get it." I know that it is true but never understood how it worked. Too many times in my life I have asked for certain things only to be very disappointed when they finally arrived.

For the first fifteen years of our marriage, my husband traveled the world as a photographer and writer. He would return home with magnificent tales and pictures of exciting adventures. I was home by myself with two small children, working in a job that I hated. His life seemed very glamorous compared to mine. I would be eating peanut-butter-and-jelly sandwiches with the kids while he was trying sushi in Japan. My dream was to travel with him. The opportunity finally came when he was traveling the West Coast one summer to photograph a book about rivers for National Geographic Books. We were all so excited as we headed out in our little Nissan pulling a pop-up camper loaded with two kids and a lot of stuff.

We went to some pretty interesting places, but it didn't take long to tire of driving long hours and setting up the camper only to take it down early the next morning and drive some more. More often than not we were camping in very remote places on the West Coast. Some of the worst moments for me were when there were no toilet facilities and we had to resort to Mother Nature. I discovered you have to examine your chosen spots beforehand very thoroughly for bugs and other creatures that fly and jump. Steve would take off in the car in the morning to shoot a sight and return that evening. That might sound exciting to you, but being left all day with two young kids and a puppy we picked up in Washington State wasn't fun. Have you ever tried to fry chicken in the kitchen of a pop-up camper?

In one place we had to be flown into the Bitterroot Wilderness of Montana in a small plane along with our supplies. We bathed in a glacier river (only once that week) and had to walk half a mile for our water. Moose, bears, and other small animals would often stop by our tents and make deposits. By the time we got out of there, I was regretting my request. Needless to say, I was not a "happy camper."

At the end of our 12,000-mile trip, I had decided that I never wanted to travel with my husband again and I never wanted to camp again, either. The pop-up camper was sold very cheaply to the first person expressing some interest. I thought it would be glamorous to travel and share his exciting experiences. But I discovered that he forgot to tell me just how hard he worked on these assignments. He forgot to share the difficult times where he didn't eat or sleep regularly. Consequently, the trip didn't look a thing like I thought it would. Only in the last few years have I been able to look fondly on that summer.

So we do get what we ask for, it just doesn't tend to look like what we expected. Yet our thoughts are an important part of that process. Edison didn't expect to create the perfect lightbulb the first time he tried. All his inventions started with a single thought and only after many attempts eventually grew into the end product we know. We forget that sometimes this creating must travel in many circles before it becomes productive.

Everything around us in our lives travels in circles. The sun, the moon, the seasons, living and dying, even history, all seem to travel in circles. And so, creating must also travel in these circles. Every thought you have leaves your mind, usually attracts similar thoughts from others, and returns to you much stronger. All of this can happen without your even opening your mouth. It's much like the frequencies a TV or radio station might send. The naked eye can't see the frequency waves, but it certainly can see the TV program, and your ears can hear the radio station. With your thoughts, certain people would turn on their mental radio to your station and pick up your signal and return a stronger signal to you. If you can understand this is what's happening constantly to everyone, then you might begin to understand why certain things happen to you.

CHALLENGE:

This exercise demonstrates how we are connected. Take a moment and think of someone you haven't talked to or seen in a while that you would like to hear from. Spend maybe a few minutes thinking about them and ask them to call you or come by in your thoughts. See how long it takes them to do it. They will probably tell you they had been thinking about you too.

It's very important to also recognize that there is a sense of order to everything. The fact that everything you think, say, or do returns to you in a circle is part of this order. It should make you feel good, because there is a system in place in which it doesn't matter if you are bad or good, young or old, rich or poor, or even what you believe. It is the same for everyone and everything that's part of creation itself. This Universal Law that states that creating must go in circles also states there have to be the consequences in the circle of things. That is part of the order to things. The return of the circle is your consequences. Contrary to popular belief, these consequences are not meant to be punishment. Their purpose is to make you aware of what you are creating and help you decide if this is what you want. We call it punishment when it isn't what we requested or when it doesn't seem fair.

Let's stop right here. Most people do not believe that they could always get what they think about or ask for. That's usually the first question I get when I'm speaking about these laws. "If this is true and I create in circles, why didn't I receive what I asked for?" Take a minute and think about the last time you really asked for something. Did you visualize what it would look like? Did you have a certain time it needed to happen? Did you have certain conditions surrounding it? Did you ever think the thought that just maybe it wouldn't happen or couldn't happen to you?

CHALLENGE:

Watch how you create by starting with something small. Take someone who really bothers you at work or at home. Make it a point to say something nice to them for several days. Watch their attitude change.

The laws do work. We are the culprits who usually stop them from working for us in a productive way. We limit how they should come to us, or what they are supposed to be. We even tend to limit the time we allow God or the universe to give them to us. How do we do this? Through thoughts, of course.

Most of us are aware of times in our lives when the same things seem to keep happening to us. It may be you find you have surrounded yourself with the same kind of people in similar relationships. Maybe you tend to be the one who tries to please others, but end up pleasing no one. Or you find yourself in stressful financial situations that seem to constantly dead-end. Whatever it is, you can usually spot it when it reappears in your life for the hundredth time. There are two ways to look at it. Either you might have been the one doing something to cause it, or it's something or someone else's fault.

Having worked with victims most of my career, I can usually spot where they are in the process. Victims feel they have no power at all. Whatever has been done has been done to them, not by them. They didn't ask for it to happen and didn't deserve for it to happen. It's always somebody else's fault.

To get them to take even some responsibility for the situation they are in is difficult. I have tremendous compassion for someone in pain. But I have come to realize (the hard way of course) that I can't make these victims change their lives or even be happy. Often they really don't want to understand it; they just want a quick fix or sympathy. I have learned that I can't force anyone to recognize his or her own power. Each person has to accept it for him or herself. These things happen to us in life to help us to see that we can change things, not to punish us or make us miserable. But to many people the word "powerful" just doesn't apply to them. I have used the word in support groups and then watched the blank faces that didn't have a clue what I was talking about.

The act of accepting your power is definitely your decision. You get to choose. When something happens to you, you can see it as punishment or a chance to discover a small part of your fantastic power. The key is in how you view it. I read in the newspaper every day about people who are in a desperate situation but use it to their benefit. For instance, you might see one person in the paper who has been diagnosed with a terminal disease decide to live life to its fullest and even help others. Then you might see another person who just gives up because they think they can't do anything about it. It's all in how you choose to look at it. If you are unable to see yourself with the power you need to make choices, no one else can give it to you.

Finances

One of the most difficult circles for most of us to understand deals with finances. Just about everyone has experienced a big gap between their checkbook and their bills at some time in their lives. This has been a difficult one for me as well. I took over the checkbook and bills very early in the marriage. I came into the relationship with parents who argued often over money because they were trying to raise five kids on a limited budget. So I was very sensitive about money to start with.

Even when my husband was working full time for a local newspaper, we never seemed to have enough money. Then when he was offered an opportunity to go to India with the minister of our church for a month, our life changed. Our daughter was only six weeks old and I had never written a check in my life. I learned very quickly what I needed to do. He came back a month later and told me he was going to quit his job at the paper and start traveling the world. I laughed at his humor, thinking it was a joke. He did quit the next week and started traveling the world. Because he has been a self-employed writer and photographer most of our thirty-three years of marriage, our finances have gone from zero to a lot. For many years I thought prayer alone would do it. Of course, we were both working and trying to make a living, but it usually wasn't enough.

What I can tell you for certain is that this law works. We have personally tested it time after time. I remember one Christmas when we had little food and no tree. Relatives unexpectedly came by with a bag of food and a Christmas tree. They didn't know what we needed, but the universe did. It just so happened they were compassionate and listening to their intuition and knew what to bring. Many other times in our life we have received money, furniture, or even cars from many different ways when we have asked for them.

If you sit down to write out your bills with dread or fear, then you are creating a circle of less money.

If you have resentment when you pay for something, you are creating a circle of less money.

If you feel guilt after buying something, you are creating a circle of less.

If you fear not having enough when it comes to your finances, then you are creating a circle of less money.

How you view it is how it comes back to you.

You might ask, "How can I approach paying my bills with a positive attitude when I don't have anything in the bank?" If you are looking at those numbers in front of you as all you have, then you are limiting what God can do. How big do you think the Universal Bank is? Is there a limit on what you can get from it? If you think your bank account, your weekly paycheck, or your investments are all that you have, then you have basically cut up your credit card to the Universal Bank.

The way to get it back is to first know and see that there is much more available to you than what you see in front of you. If you believe your account is just a place for money to flow through from lots of different sources, then it is. This really isn't very different when you look at the numbers in your checkbook or when you get your investment statement. You trust that the bank or the stockbroker is giving you the right numbers. You don't know—they could have made a mistake or be lying. It's really a piece of paper with numbers on it. Do you actually touch or count the money? Probably not. You write more numbers on pieces of paper called checks or you charge things from a card. What creates it for you is the fact that you believe you have earned it and it's yours. This works the same way. What you choose to believe in and trust is what you get. It's the belief in a system that isn't limited to what's right in front of you or what you can see with your eyes.

You might say that you've never been given anything in life but what you have earned. Are you really saying that no one has ever given you even a dollar? Or maybe you have never found or won something? You've never been given a gift of some sort? Money can come to you in many ways, not just through your job. Don't limit it.

CHALLENGE:

While you are paying your bills for just one month, try to pay them with joy. See the money going out and touching other people like yourself, not just big companies. It provides these people with a living so they can take care of their families. See what comes back.

The law says, "If you simply know that everything you need is taken care of, and let the universe bring it back to you, you will have enough." This sounds too simple, but it isn't. It takes a lot of strength to know that this or that bill will be paid even when the money isn't in the bank. This doesn't mean you just sit and wait. Of course you work and look at options that might come to you. But the key is to allow the universe to give you what you need. Don't limit how it comes or what it's supposed to look like. Maybe it will come as a hand-me-down from someone. Or maybe you will be able to barter for what you want.

CHALLENGE:

Another way to test your financial possibilities is to give a part of your monthly income to a charity, nonprofit, or some other organization that needs help. You get to determine how much, but it's important to give willingly. This act of kindness is saying that you believe the universe will take care of all of your needs.

Also, just watch your thoughts so they don't stop the process or slow it down by using "can't," "shouldn't," "wouldn't," or "impossible." These words literally bring everything to a halt. If you find that you're thinking such thoughts, change them to ones that acknowledge that anything is possible. See money as a green piece of paper that is there to help you figure out that you have the power to control it, not the opposite. Ask for your needs or wants and then let go. Send out your bills with joy, knowing that others will receive their paychecks because you did. Know that you are not reducing the money in your account, but simply releasing some to the rest of the universe. It has to come back in even larger quantities.

When you re-create your views on finances, you are consciously choosing to see them from a different position. The more things that can leave your mind with joy and thanks, the more you're going to get back. Not just in money or things, but as if to say, "This doesn't own me anymore. Money isn't powerful, I am." You're entitled; it's your inheritance. Remember, though, that anyone can take an inheritance and squander it.

It's your choice and your lesson.

Steps to Change Your Finances

1) Find a quiet place and try to let go of all your worries or concerns of the day.

2) Take a moment to create the picture you want your finances to look like. Maybe it's a bank vault filled to the top with all the money you need.

3) See money coming to you from different sources, not just your job. Don't stay too long on where it comes from—just see yourself making deposits.

4) Next, see yourself writing checks for your bills with joy, not fear or resentment. For every dollar you send out, see two returning.

5) See that money going out and benefiting many people in that circle. For example, the company that gets it, then pays its employees, who take it to buy groceries or clothes.

6) Finally, see the money return to you doubled and give thanks to the universe. Always give thanks, no matter what the situation looks like.

7) Every time the fear of not having enough money attacks you—STOP. Replace that fear with the circle of plenty you want to create.

CHAPTER 4

The Law of Cause and Effect

Have you ever been watching a horror movie and seen the character doing something you think is stupid? You're sitting there and what they've done makes absolutely no sense to you. You know when they open that door, or get in the car with the murderer, something is going to happen to them. Sitting there in your den or in the movie theater, you can easily see what is going to happen when they make those bad choices. It's pretty easy for us to see everyone else's poor choices, but not our own.

This law is about choices and their consequences. Each of us has choices every minute of every day. As we said before, you create in circles, which means that whatever you have created comes back to you. We have also said that when it comes back to you, it is not punishment. Instead, it is for you to have the opportunity to recognize it and make choices. You probably will either keep it the same, change it to something different, or release it.

The most comfortable choice is the one of least resistance. This means you will most likely keep doing the same old things or stay in the same patterns and send them right back out. Often you either don't see any other choices or you simply try to ignore whatever is in front of you. One strong example of this could be the arguments we have with each other in relationships. I used to say you could just play a tape of the arguments between my husband and myself. They were always the same. One of us would start with a statement or accusation and the other would respond exactly as they had done hundreds of times. I used to joke about playing tape #1 about money or #2 about relatives when we were arguing. It wasn't much fun, but at least I knew what was coming. We simply weren't aware that we could change things.

Another choice would be to change the situation. The first step to doing this is to decide to see this very old issue differently. This is also where most people have to get discouraged enough or frustrated enough to be willing to try something new. I have a friend who had worked her way up in the banking industry for eighteen years. For the last several years she had been complaining that she hated her job and wanted something new. She didn't see how that could happen when banking was all she knew. Once in a while she would look for other jobs, but she didn't feel qualified for anything else. Finally one day she had enough and just quit her job. She was able to get a job with a nonprofit organization that had some accounting duties, but also enabled her to provide counseling and other support services to others in distress.

Once she changed how she viewed her qualifications, she was able to change jobs.

Finally, you could actually choose to release this thing that keeps returning to you. Most of the time this doesn't happen until you have worked through that circle many times. Usually you have to reach a point where you are willing to just let it go. It could be a relationship, a harmful habit, or even the fear of something. When it no longer has a hold on you emotionally, you can know it's probably gone. It still might show up from time to time, but you won't react to it the same way, so it won't demand your attention.

CHALLENGE:

To start with something small, pick something you hate to do but seem to get stuck with all the time. See yourself saying, "No, not this time." See someone else doing it and everyone being fine. It's important not to feel guilty about this. You will notice the world goes on even if you do say "No." You are taking back your own power.

The bottom line is you always have choices. We start having choices even before we are born. We get to choose our parents and what we want to work on in that lifetime. We also get to choose the people we want to be around. People find this incredible, but it is the truth. You choose your parents and family, who drive you crazy, to help you to remember what it is you need to remember. Usually they have traits or characteristics that you do not like about yourself. Since we share these traits, we tend to drive each other crazy. But they are teachers. They also are usually people we have old connections with, so they are "safe."

CHALLENGE:

Choose to do something you've always wanted to do for yourself. Give yourself a treat, whatever that is for you. If you continue only giving to others and not yourself, you will eventually feel resentful and drained. You will realize that as you feel better, your circles will feel better. Don't wait for others to give you permission.

Sometimes these choices we make about our families don't seem to make sense. As adults we forget why we agreed to come and what we are here for. A question I often hear is people asking why a child would consciously choose a parent or family that is going to abuse or even kill him.

First, children are given lots of chances to leave the situation, a lot more than adults. Many children have died from crib death without medical explanation. It wasn't the parent's fault. The soul just decided to return to heaven for personal reasons. I am not trying to insinuate that every parent who has lost a child has been a bad parent. Quite the contrary, many are great parents. But even though the soul is in a very tiny, helpless body, it gets a choice too. Children come and go so much in their dreams. They don't stay in the body all the time, especially within the first three years.

These children get to change their minds because sometimes the sheer act of being born creates a whole potential path that they are not ready for. Or maybe just being born and affecting other people's lives was all they actually had to do. It would be very much like if you went to the grocery store, realized you forgot your list, and went home to get it. They get here and realize, "I need a few more classes. I'm just not ready to stay right now. I think I'll go back." And they do. Some of the greatest changes that have occurred in our laws have happened due to a parent's crusade after a child's death. Maybe all that child agreed to do was spend some time with the parents and in death motivate them to create these changes in the system, thus fulfilling part of the purpose in their life.

Another answer might be that there is something going on between the child and the parents that is very old. Perhaps they have agreed to work out some old debt through the abuse. Of course all parties get to make different choices, so they can achieve the results they want through other ways. But usually if the situation was very emotional originally, the parties involved need to reconnect with those old emotions to deal with it. Perhaps the child was the parent the last time. If the child was extremely abusive to his or her children, he or she may have decided the best way to learn would be to experience abuse firsthand. We don't ever know, so it's hard to judge what we can't see. But I have always found it very interesting that most of the abused children I have worked with wanted to stay with their abusive parent or parents. Sometimes it's very hard to accept the fact that these magnificent beings in little bodies are choosing, too.

I did my internship in graduate school in a low-income housing project in North Carolina. I provided counseling and other assistance to several thirteen-year-old mothers and sixteen-year-old addicts. After school a group of us tutored children of all ages. One face that often comes to my mind is that of a seven-year-old girl I had worked with. After several months of counseling, she began to tell me about different situations in her home. Her drawings said what her mouth couldn't. She had five brothers and sisters and each had a different father. She didn't like her mother's current boyfriend, but felt she needed to be near her mother to protect her. We suspected her mother's boyfriend was molesting her, and I had to report the suspicions to child protective services. Her mother ran the boyfriend off during the investigation, but let him return as soon as it was over. The young lady was no longer allowed to visit me for counseling sessions, but I did see her on the playground one day. She was upset that I reported her and had betrayed her confidence. She told me that she would never leave her mother and neither I nor anyone else could make her hate her mother.

It was hard to make sense out of the different things I saw and felt. But I do know that that child had a connection to her mother. I saw the poverty and abuse, but she saw it as all she had known and it was her family. Children have a whole lot more going for them that you cannot see, particularly if their situation looks unjust. If you see them as just tiny little people who are totally dependent on adults, you are not seeing the whole picture. This doesn't mean that we aren't supposed to help or get involved in the situation when we can. It's saying that we should try to see more of the picture before judging it.

So back to the question, "Why would a child choose to be hurt or even killed?" Or even better, "Why does the Creator allow children to be hurt and killed?" The answer would be choices. The Creator has set up a system of order where you get to have choices before birth and certainly from the first second of birth. Everyone involved has choices. Of course at any time any of the parties involved can choose to change things. They don't have to hurt each other again to learn something.

CHALLENGE:

The next time you are in a good mood and someone comes along and is nasty to you, don't let them spoil your day. You can choose to react emotionally, but don't accept it. Don't stay in the emotions, trying to figure out why they were nasty to you. Just see the nastiness going back to its creator. In doing this, you are consciously releasing the insult and creating different circles.

If just one person tries to change himself or herself, he or she will affect everyone else involved. Remember, you can't really change anyone else, only yourself. Know that when you try to make these changes, the people around you are going to react. There's a good possibility that their reactions won't be positive ones. They might say things like: "You've changed. You're different. You think you are better than everyone else." What they are really saying is they are uncomfortable because now they have to change the way they react to you. If you become a more assertive person, they won't like it because they can't control you anymore. If the change involved your being more happy or positive, they might not like that, either. But you are not doing this for them; hopefully you are doing this for yourself. The very best way to help people is to simply try to live your own life the best way you can. You'll always have an audience and the ones most critical are the ones most interested.

How to Change Your Choices

1) When you feel a strong emotion such as anger, frustration, sadness, or being trapped—simply STOP. Know that you are simply at the beginning of the circle again.

2) Get in a quiet place and take a few moments to look at what is going on. Try to see all sides of whatever is affecting you.

3) Go backward and see how you could have created the situation. Have you simply reacted the same way you always have?

4) How would you like to change it? What would you like to see different about it?

5) What choices do you have in front of you?

6) See yourself choosing one of these choices in your head and look at the possible end results of this choice.

7) Remember that old patterns are the easiest to follow, and that change can be difficult and feel uncomfortable.

8) See yourself successfully completing whatever choice you make.

9) To release it—see whatever it is as a small bird in your hands. Just let it go and know you don't have to have control over it anymore. Watch the bird fly away.

CHAPTER 5

Everything in Creation Has Opposites

Let's imagine for a moment that opposites don't exist in your world and everything is the same. You wake up at exactly the same time every day. You fix your coffee and eat the same food for breakfast that you always do. You dress in the same outfit and leave your home for work at exactly the same time each morning. As you walk out to your car, you see all your neighbors leaving the exact same time and dressed the exact same way you are. Traveling down the highway toward work, you notice that all the other cars are exactly like yours and everyone is going at the same speed. You get to work, where everyone talks and acts the same and performs the same tasks, day after day. There are very few stimulating conversations during the day because everyone thinks alike, so they already agree with each other. Does this sound a little too perfect to you?

If you really thought about it, life without opposites would be quite boring. Yet, we tend to divide everything and everyone into just two categories, good and bad. We think we want to eliminate all of the bad and only have the good. Just like the example we just looked at, only good would eventually be very boring to us. The truth is you can't just divide everything into good and bad. But since we have a tendency to try to control everything around us, we divide everything and everyone into categories. To make this seem more real, if we convince most of the people to agree on what is good and what is bad, then life will work much more predictably.

Life isn't that simple. We aren't supposed to be homogenized. There are opposites of everything in nature for a purpose. Take water, for example. The entire world, including animals and plant life, needs water to exist. Yet too much water causes flooding, which ruins crops, destroys homes, and drowns people and animals. We also need the sun to exist, yet too much can cause cancer in humans. I have discovered through various Indian medicine women that most of the healing plants and roots used have twin plants that are very poisonous. These women spend a long time training to be able to identify the differences.

Let's look at ourselves. We have a right and a left hand, which are opposites. We have a right eye and left eye. The left and right sides of our brains control the entire body. Usually these sides work together to help us think, talk, walk, eat, and generally function. They aren't "bad" or "good," they just complement each other. We usually don't think too much about it until something doesn't seem to be working for us or becomes ill. But the truth is, just as our bodies are opposites that complement, so are our souls. To be complete and perfect, you have to have both sides—the knowing and the unknowing.

CHALLENGE:

Watch the news or read the paper and note how often they use words that tend to divide. What are they trying to convince you of? Do you agree with them?

This law is attempting to help you understand that we aren't divided and therefore can't be placed into little compartments. We are whole, complete beings just like the rest of the universe around us. We just choose to look at one part or another. So this whole idea is not about fixing anything. It's not about labeling anything. It's about how you perceive yourself and the world around you. The best place to start changing your perceptions is with yourself. You are a perfect reproduction of everything in the universe. Therefore, you have to have opposites inside of you in order to balance and complete that wholeness.

You don't have good and bad parts or even strengths and weaknesses. You simply have within you one part that complements the other. The only way to look at this is to see the whole, not the sections. Would you want your friends or coworkers to see you in the first ten minutes after waking in the morning and decide that's who you really are? No, you wouldn't. Most of us would prefer to get showered and dressed before we are seen. Yet when we make a decision about another person or an action that is "bad" or "good," we have done just that. We are saying they belong to one category or another based on the few moments we have interacted with them.

CHALLENGE:

When you hear someone else at work or home use these words, stop them and ask what makes the things so "good" or "bad." (Be prepared for them to accuse you of being a little crazy.)

That means you have to do away with your labels and criticism. Instead, you have to be more understanding and accepting of all parts of others and particularly with yourself. That's hard, because we tend to be our worst and most critical enemies. How many times a day do you criticize your own actions or thoughts? Most of the time we aren't even aware of what we are doing. We just do it. We are so quick to condemn, but unbelievably slow to praise ourselves. It's interesting that the very things you probably criticize yourself for are the very things about you that make you unique. I notice that my granddaughter can spill her milk and I will quickly reassure her that everything is fine—it's just milk. If I spill or drop something, I am calling myself clumsy for at least several hours.

Instead of identifying these opposites as "good" and "bad," we can call these parts the knowing side or the unknowing side. There is no judgment to this kind of identification. The knowing part of you not only feels connected to your Creator but also allows you to explore new thoughts and ideas. It's the part that reacts with compassion and love to others. The unknowing part is afraid of change and allows you to feel anger, frustration, or fear. It constantly questions and allows you to explore areas that don't feel so good. Since questioning, fear, and anger are motivators for change, they are very necessary. They are as important to the growth process as understanding. Just as a beautiful flower needs both the sun and rain to grow, you need both joy and anger to grow.

CHALLENGE:

Take some quiet time and examine the last few times you have called your thoughts, words, or actions "good" or "bad." Could you use some other words to describe them other than these two? Maybe you could try to see if you can relate how they would be coming from the knowing or unknowing side of you.

It's very much like a car. That car has many parts that not only complement each other, but have to work together. You have right and left headlights, front and back seats. You also have many other parts under the hood that can't be divided easily into right and left but still complement each other. When everything is working together, the car runs with few or no problems. If there is a problem, it usually affects the other parts around it. For instance, if the starter switch isn't getting the charge it needs to start the engine, the car doesn't go anywhere. Many a time we have taken our cars into the shop to be fixed only to have something else go wrong in a day or two. The mechanics would say that it wasn't what they worked on, but something else around the broken area.

That's what we are like. We are complex beings with many parts that work together. To label the engine as bad and the air filter as good would not be helpful if you were trying to fix the car. The mechanic needs to find what parts are not working at their best and replace or fix them. We, as humans, get stuck in that process when we stay in the emotions of simply reacting. When we label our words, thoughts, or actions as good or bad, we are just stuck. It's like standing there with the hood open and not having a clue where to find the problem. When you think something isn't working, you just want to jerk it out and everything around it. That kind of attitude won't help your car work properly and certainly won't help you, either.

This means if you criticize or label yourself for something you said or thought or did, you are simply standing there with the hood up jerking out parts. If you can get out of the habit of labeling yourself, then you can examine where it came from and why. Even when you are hurtful or spiteful to others, it just means that something in you was touched enough to react. It's an indication that some parts aren't working together the way they could and need to be checked. It certainly doesn't qualify you as "good" or "bad."

CHALLENGE:

List four of your strengths on one side of a piece of paper and four weaknesses on the other side. Try to connect the opposites that seem to balance out each other by drawing lines. What makes them "good" or "bad"? Don't spend more than five or ten minutes doing this.

What about Killing Others?

You might be asking if there is no good or bad, then what about people killing or harming each other? How could a brutal killing be called simply unknowing? Don't get me wrong. I am not advocating that people should hurt each other. Those who hurt others are certainly creating their own circles that will return. There will be an effect from those actions that will return to that person. But even in death people have choices. It isn't the end. There is a continuation of the soul, which has the opportunity to review the life and decide whether to come back or not. Consequently, it isn't the death we want to focus on, but the living of the life.

We've been taught that "good" Christian people who live their lives being kind and giving to others should receive a quick, painless death in old age as part of their reward. We also tend to believe that "bad" people deserve to be put in prison or die slow, painful deaths. We get very upset if a "good" person unjustly receives a premature or horrible death by someone else's hand. We as a culture have very definite ideas how life and death are supposed to be. Yet, just about everyone I've talked to states they want to die by falling asleep in old age.

If you are going to accept these beliefs, I would ask you is there anyone who is totally good or totally bad? If not, then obviously the term is earned by the number or types of words or deeds performed in one's life. So how many things do people need to do or say to be considered "good" or "bad"? Who's going to judge if you performed enough "good" deeds to deserve a painless death or enough "bad" ones to die a slow death? Whoever it is will have to watch and know your every thought, word, and deed. To add yet more confusion, what one person might describe as good another might not. The reality is most of us try to do the best we can and hope for some leniency when we seem to fail.

If you can release the terms "good" and "bad" and see yourself as having knowing and unknowing parts, then you don't have to judge how you should live or die. Again, I am not advocating that people hurt or kill each other. But somewhere we have to start to understand that there is much more to all of this than we want to recognize. Life isn't just about working, living, and dying. I hear people asking all the time,

"What is this all about?" It's about discovering the opposites in ourselves through each other and allowing them to work together. If you stay focused on something "bad" that has happened to you or someone you love, then you are only seeing part of the picture. Try looking at the "good" in your life and see the whole picture.

CHALLENGE:

Look at a person who has hurt you or who you are angry with. Can you list their strengths and weaknesses as you see them? How does their list compare to yours? Do you share any of their qualities? If you can release some of the emotions, ask, "What was this whole experience for me to learn about?" After you ask the question, write down everything you hear in your thoughts. Don't stop and don't question it. You'll get your answer.

We are here by our choice, doing what we have chosen to do. Even if the decisions don't seem to be conscious, you still chose them for very good reasons. This is how we can discover the pain of death and the joy of love. In that process, we are able to recognize not only our connection to the Creator and the rest of creation, but also how we are interwoven with everything and everyone else around us. That spider you step on or that bug you kill is just as much a part of the Creator as you. It has a purpose in creation and it fulfills it. We kill it because it makes us afraid or interferes with our homes and lives. Often we kill each other for the same reasons.

So back to the answer of the question concerning how a loving God could create or even allow murder, molestation, violence, and crime. God created opposites to balance each other. God also created beings that were partners in creating. These creatures also have choices. In their creating they are allowed to choose what they want in order to understand both.

What about Heaven or Hell?

So if God created opposites, then there must be a heaven and a hell. I know I'm going to get quite a bit of resistance in saying this, but there is no hell. Heaven isn't a place where angels strum their harps and float around all the time, either. How do I know? Of course I do remember what my last experience was while I was in a place called heaven. I have received quite a lot of information from angels concerning this place. Also I have seen and talked to many people who are dead and for some of them they are pretty sure they are in hell.

Even in death we have our knowing and unknowing parts. Even in death you make choices. The life experiences and memories that you bring with you at dying either keep you stuck on Earth or allow you to go to a place of learning called heaven. Some spirits that I have talked to were stuck because they were angry with someone or felt they had been treated unjustly. Others thought they still needed to control their business or families. Still others either didn't know they were dead or felt they had died too early. So either unfinished business or strong emotions held them to Earth. Some people wander around thinking they deserved to be punished. If they had been cruel or harmed or killed another being, they would be tied to them after death. Most of these spirits thought they were in hell. If they are willing to move on, we can explore what it is that's holding them here in order for them to release it and go on. But never, never, have I seen or heard of the burning lake of fire that I was often threatened with while growing up.

Now the other place our spirits go to is the opposite of being stuck. It is a place of learning and joy. It is a place of pleasures and reuniting with loved ones. It is a place where we are allowed to understand what it was we were trying to do our last lifetime. There is no God on a throne who is going to judge you. Since you are cocreators with God, you get to review your lives and choose what you want to create the next time. It's also a place of relearning what you already know and expanding that knowing to learn of future things.

In this place you often get to return to loved ones that are alive when they need you. Not being stuck means you can travel back and forth freely. I would like to clarify that most beings tend to hang around their loved ones for a while after death. This does not mean they are stuck. It just means they want to make sure the loved ones are doing OK, and they might choose to try to reassure them they are doing fine. They do this by approaching you in your dreams. Or maybe you will have thoughts of them or feel them close by. They are right beside you, trying to reassure you there is an afterlife and they are fine. Most people don't trust their intuition that says this is not only possible but true. Don't cheat yourself out of the experience by simply dismissing it. Instead, acknowledge their presence and listen for a message from them that will come to you through your own thoughts.

This Universal Law is telling you that you have to have opposites. It also is saying that these opposites complement each other and work together to allow you to experience all the things you need in order to understand how complete and perfect you are.

Steps to Understand Opposites

1) Start to become aware of how often you define things as "bad" or "good." See if you can count the number of times you have used these words in a twenty-four-hour period. What were they connected with?

2) Start to be aware of conversations with other people. How often do they use these words? Did you agree with them or did you see things differently?

3) The next time you criticize yourself—STOP. Think about the situation. Instead, see the opposite trait in yourself. See the traits as balanced and praise yourself.

4) If all else fails, visualize yourself as a car. When you are being critical of yourself, you are jerking out parts you need to operate. Instead, see yourself under the hood asking what part or parts need your attention.

CHAPTER 6

There Are No Judgments—Only Lessons

It's interesting that we humans are the only beings on Earth that judge. Animals don't judge each other; they simply use their instincts. Plants don't judge each other; neither do the stars or the moon. Why do we do that? Is it a feeble attempt to explain why things happen or is it our way to control our world? This Universal Law is saying that the Creator doesn't judge us in any way. If God created us perfect, then why would there be a need for judgment or punishment?

Reward/Punishment System

I remember several spankings I received while growing up that I felt didn't fit the crime. My parents trained me well to the benefits of the punishment and reward system, but often

I tested it anyway. One of the worst spankings I remember was when my dad caught my younger brother and me climbing on the roof of a house that was being built in our neighborhood. It was framed in, but not enclosed, so we were walking only on the beams. We thought it was a great adventure and had no second thoughts concerning danger. Anyway, we were showing off to several of the younger neighborhood children, so any potential danger was worth it.

Out of the corner of my eye I saw a car abruptly stop in the middle of the road. "Somebody recognizes how brave we are," I thought to myself. To my horror my dad jumped out of the car, hollering at us. I suddenly realized we might have gone too far. He waited as we slowly crawled down and we rode the rest of the trip home in silence. That evening he gave me a spanking I will never forget. Being the oldest of five children I was expected to be a good role model and not lead them into danger. Even later when he tried to talk to me about it, I didn't think it was fair. I didn't feel I had done anything wrong. Other kids got into a lot more trouble than we did, so I felt he should be grateful. We weren't drinking or using drugs. He didn't see my point then and it took many years for me to understand his.

In the beginning of time, when the Creator first planted human beings, it was important for each spirit to recognize what he or she had created. Consequently, the Universal Laws of "Creating in Circles" and "Cause and Effect" were included as a way for us to do this. Whatever was created returned to its creator much stronger than it was originally. This meant that whenever someone thought, said, or did something, it would return to them with much more energy than it left. But when those things returned to humans that involved pain or suffering, they needed an explanation. As people tried to explain life's ups and downs, the opposites were labeled as "bad" and "good," leading to "punishment" and "reward."

Throughout the centuries, many rules have been conceived in an attempt to define exactly what those terms meant. That way we could know if we were pleasing God or not by the end results. If God answered your prayers, then you were a "good" person who followed the rules and were therefore "rewarded." If God didn't answer those prayers, or more "bad" things happened to you, then you were most certainly being "punished." If you needed to explain "bad" things happening to a "good" person, then it was decided that God was testing them. Various quotes from the book of Job in the Bible have provided inspiration for this belief.

In spite of these rules, most of our attempts to please God and receive our reward end up with us falling on our faces. Consequently, we find ourselves returning to God constantly asking forgiveness for something we have said, done, or thought. Growing up as a Baptist meant that every so often I would rededicate my life to God. Afterward, I would feel light and happy for several days until I realized I had broken another rule. With a heavy heart, I would start the process all over again. It felt like I was trying to climb a spiritual ladder to God. I would only reach the second or third step when I would fall and have to start all over at the bottom.

These Universal Laws free you from these rigid rules in several ways. First and most important, God is always with you. The Creator never turns Their back on you, much less leaves you. All God wants to do is help you to recognize that you are a partner in creation.

Second, God loves you so much that when you were created, everything else in the universe was created to help you. Every intricate part of the universe fits together. The more I watch the Discovery Channel programs and learn about all these parts of nature, the more I am in awe of how the Creator thought of everything. We have food, water, the sun, and the moon. We have pleasure and love as well as pain and death. It's all there for us. The sunsets that absolutely take your breath are there for your pleasure and enjoyment. The fragrance of a beautiful flower is there to please your nose. The stars twinkle and the moon glows for us to see and enjoy as well as affect the ebb and flow of the tides.

Third, to create order and help us discover our own power, a system of Universal Laws was put into place. These weren't laws or rules that could be broken, but were really a blueprint for the order that encompassed the entire universe. These laws weren't based on "bad" or "good" or "punishment" and "reward." Instead they allowed us the freedom to choose knowing there are no wrong choices. There are only various opportunities to learn how to use this power we have. So there is no win or lose in this system; there are only lessons.

You are allowed to create the same thing many times to help you eventually decide to change it. This isn't a system where if you don't get it the third time you're going to be sent to hell. What if it's part of the universal system to learn about creating and enjoying life through those things you call "mistakes?" They usually are the very things that stick in our mind. You always have choices. If you had thirty people visiting a beautiful garden, everyone wouldn't look at the same thing the whole time. Some people might really be taken with the tulips and someone else might like the trees, a rock, or even a mushroom. So when we make choices and revisit the same place, it's as if we are standing there in that garden just staring at that flower, tree, or mushroom. There's nothing wrong with it; it's just your way of learning.

You are infatuated with it, that's all. Once you have seen it enough, you will move on to something else. Who am I or anyone else to tell you what to look at and for how long?

There's no judgment to this way of learning. Yet our very first reaction when we see the same thing happening over and over is to kick ourselves or start blaming something or someone. We think we have failed. This law is saying you can't fail. You are just staring at that flower or mushroom a little while longer.

How you learn is unique to you. You might think that you have stepped forward and then gone backward. What you've done is learn your own way. Somebody else might do it a different way.

The group of people that was formed to develop this material was a perfect example. It was fascinating to watch the different ways a group of people can learn over a year. When a new law was discussed, various group members would ask questions. As they left for the night, each person would have a different idea of how this law applied to their life. The next week we would discuss what had happened to them over the previous week that related to the law. It was obvious that some people learned by simply holding their noses and jumping in. They would incorporate the new idea and make changes immediately in their life without testing it. Often, though, others tested and retested it with coworkers, family, or friends. Then if it seemed to work, they noted the changes.

Still others sat back and questioned as they listened. They wouldn't think of jumping into something until they were sure it worked. These folks were the skeptics and would passionately argue their point of view. Until they saw huge changes in other group members, they wouldn't consider trying it for themselves. All the group members were each other's teachers.

Judging Others

One of the easiest things to do is to judge someone else. It just sort of slips out of your mouth or pops in your head. We all do it. We judge each other by our body builds, skin colors, clothes we wear, places we live, cars we drive, things we say, and the attitudes we have. All of these things are our differences. It's interesting that everyone wants to be unique, but also wants to look, act, and talk like everyone else. Have you ever caught yourself judging someone only later to find out that you were totally wrong?

The most obvious way we judge each other is through observation or gossip. It is so ingrained in us that our minds are constantly sizing up other people around us. Gossip tends to show up in even the most innocent of conversations. What we're really doing when we gossip is trying to fit people into categories. We are also trying to gain acceptance from some people by noticing things about others we don't like. We can convince ourselves that we are in the group that has it all. We don't have these characteristics, so we must be better than they are.

Again, we're back to the idea of people seeing you the first thing in the morning. What if you woke up tomorrow morning and found all your coworkers or friends just standing around your bed staring at you? You'd probably be horrified. Yet, whenever you are gossiping about someone, that's exactly what you're doing. You are taking a few moments or hours that you are around them and deciding that's who they are all the time. Even children judge each other. They can be quite hurtful too. Where did they learn to do this? By watching and listening to their older family members and others around them. If they are that good at it when they are young, how much better will they be when they become adults?

For those people who think observations aren't judging, think again. I would ask you, "If they knew what you were saying about them in the observation, would their feelings be hurt?" If so, then it's harmful and judging. All of this, whether it's gossip or observations, leaves your head or mouth and returns to you much stronger. Is that what you want to create?

CHALLENGE:

Try to catch yourself the next time you are tempted to gossip or even listen to it. See the words going out of the mouth and touching the person you are talking about. They will know someone is talking about them because the words have energy. When you first hear them in your head or coming out of your mouth—STOP. See yourself in your bed first thing in the morning and all these people gossiping about you standing at your bed. What do you think they would say about you? How does that feel? Try to turn the gossip into a compliment or just keep quiet.

Since we are such creative beings, how we learn and how we see will be very individual and different. In other words, we are supposed to be different. I don't think I could live with four other people that looked like me, talked like me, or thought like me. But for some reason we think that everyone should understand or agree with us all of the time. Life would get pretty boring if that were so.

I went with a friend to a craft fair one time. I naturally gravitate toward the pottery. I love all types of pottery, but particularly things that are functional. This one artist had about forty coffee cups lying in boxes under the tables. I asked him if they were for sale. He told me that they were his rejects and I could take all I wanted. (Of course I took as many as my arms could carry, but I paid him) Not one of those cups was identical to another. The ones on top of the table that were perfect didn't look exactly alike, either. Even if that artist tried he couldn't make each cup exactly identical.

We are supposed to be very different from each other. That's what makes the Creator happy. Actually those individual characteristics that you have are the way God identifies you. That means that not only is it great to be different, but we're supposed to share with each other, just not compare. When you start comparing your life or your experiences with the idea that yours is best, you are judging.

It's very easy to judge others because we are usually just reacting out of fear. It can be the fear of being hurt, a confrontation, or even the fear of rejection. Usually there is an emotion attached that seems to allow the quick judgment to jump out even before you realize it. You might think at first that you're nothing like the person you are reacting to and judging. But sooner or later something happens that seems to push you out of your safe world. More times than not I have caught myself doing exactly what I judged someone else for earlier.

CHALLENGE:

Start being aware of your thoughts during the day. When one pops up that's critical or judging of others, ask that a flag appear to get your attention. Could the person you are criticizing possibly be your teacher or even an angel in disguise?

If we're not supposed to judge each other, what are we supposed to do with these differences? It would help if we could just enjoy and appreciate each other's differences. Sometimes those very differences are what attract us to certain people. One way that helps me is to see life as a stage. Each person is simply wearing a different costume. If you find someone in rags, that's their costume for their part of the play. Or maybe you have someone who chose stardom and wealth sitting over here with a big house. That's their part in the play! The beauty is that all parts of the Creator are so magnificent that they can't be shown through just one thing. They have to be displayed, shown, and experienced through all kinds of things, people, and situations. I know that when I'm meeting someone new, I'm getting to see another part of God I hadn't noticed before.

Another helpful way to look at these differences is that we are each other's teachers. The people who can bring up the strongest emotions in you are your teachers. Then what are they trying to show you? For each person, even the lessons being taught are different. The beauty of this whole thing is that you don't have to understand everything to be connected. Your teachers are sitting out there just as surely as the sun rises every morning. They will be there when you need them. You are affecting them too. That's why if you have a judgment or put someone in a category before you even know them, you're really doing a disservice to them and to yourself.

Our teachers don't usually look like prophets or old gray-haired men. They are probably the people you work with or play with. They probably are your family members, including your parents and children. If you are asking for patience, they will be the ones trying your patience on a regular basis. Or if your spirit needs some boosting, they will probably be the ones to say just the right thing.

Others Who Judge You

Whatever fears you are trying to conquer will shape the life situations that happen to you. Let's say you have a fear of being rejected or not having enough money, you will probably surround yourself with people who have similar fears. Then the ones who would be judging you have the same fears. You tend to rely on what the outward parts say—the mouth, the eyes, or body language. Start listening to your own gut or intuition, because often these people won't tell you what's really bothering them. When people judge you, know that the very thing they are doing is condemning themselves. Rejection is simply judgment turned around. They are not going to have a very strong reaction to you if it is not something that bothers them also. Many people are miserable in their lives or their relationships. We love to put up a front that everything is fine and you won't catch us being miserable, but people are. Listen to how they talk. Do they complain very often? Do they feel they are victims of someone else? Do they feel like life isn't treating them fairly?

Judging Yourself

If you are judging others, you are still judging yourself. The reason is you can't see anything in them you don't already have. Where you get stuck is when you criticize yourself instead of just seeing it as an opportunity to change or release something that's not working for you. That's when you add all this extra junk to it.

It's human nature to judge. You're playing a tape recorder that's inside of you and it's been there since your first minute of existence. Since most people have spent a great deal of their lives either accepting or giving criticism, those tapes are going to automatically come back and say critical things to you. These criticisms tend to come from fear or anger. For instance, if you have been destitute for three lifetimes, the emotions attached to that are going to be very strong and try to pull you back into that. So you might have the belief that you will do anything to keep from being poor this time. Or you might have a strong fear of losing your house, your things, or even food. If your peers have rejected you in the past, their opinions in this lifetime will matter a lot. You will probably spend a lot of time and energy trying to please others.

When it seems like your life is not working like it should, you immediately judge yourself. You do this by saying that you didn't do this right or didn't do that right and you've failed. You haven't failed; you're simply in the circle. If you are calling yourself names or being harsh or critical, that circle goes out and you are strengthening the very parts of yourself you dislike.

CHALLENGE:

We all tend to talk to ourselves by fussing. We say things like we are clumsy, stupid, accident prone, or just plain forgetful. When that happens, what voice are you hearing? It's probably a parent or teacher that told you these things when you were growing up. So when it happens—STOP. Turn around to the voice and tell it you are really doing pretty good. Then laugh with yourself because humor is important.

One of the most difficult areas I have had to work on is the list that's in my head. At the end of the day I would decide that if I had accomplished one-half or more of the things on my list, I had good marks for the day. If I spent the day doing something I enjoyed, like working with the flowerbeds or thrift store shopping, I would feel guilty and give myself "bad" marks for the day because I didn't accomplish anything. The list never seemed to get shorter and it didn't feel like I accomplished very much. I'm still working on this one, but I have started to realize that the day flows much better when I just make my plans and release them. If certain things happen, then that's fine. If they don't, then I look at what I got out of the day. You know, you can pull and tug all day trying to get it all done. By the end of the day you are exhausted and you're still holding onto that rope in a tug-of-war. What would happen if you quit pulling and just let it go? Balance and peacefulness take the place of frustration and exhaustion. This doesn't mean that you aren't busy, because you are. It just means that you've enjoyed whatever it was you were doing so much the day passed quickly and without effort.

Judging Your Body

I was bathing our four-year-old granddaughter recently when, to my surprise, she bowed out her chest and proudly announced that she would have big "boobies" soon. I really didn't think about her even noticing this lack of chest muscles. But as she plays with her Barbie doll, I know she notices that perfect body. If that doll doesn't get her, watching TV will. We are barraged by tiny, perfect bodies or strong, handsome male prototypes. Consequently, I am not surprised to hear one of the strongest self-criticisms concerns the body. Many people feel their body, or package as I often call it, is far less than perfect. They feel their bodies are the wrong color, the wrong size, or the wrong shape.

First, you pretty much chose your body style when you chose your parents and your lifestyle before each lifetime. Second, it helps if you could think of the body as a package, a covering. That's all it is. It houses the soul or the spirit and it's like wearing a costume on stage while in a play. Does the costume tell you who or what the actor wearing it is? No. It only describes a part in that particular play, not the being wearing it.

CHALLENGE:

To help with judging yourself, think about the first thought you have in the morning when you are looking into the mirror. What do you say to yourself? When you catch yourself moaning about your body fat or your thick thighs—STOP. Think about all the Barbie dolls lined up on the shelf. Do you really want to just blend in like the others? Then release the idea of what you think your body absolutely needs to look like. This doesn't mean you don't take care of yourself—you do; it just says you don't criticize the package you are in this time.

I've heard many single people tell me that if they don't have the right figure or clothes, the opposite sex won't be attracted to them. The clothes or the body might get other people's attention at first, but it's the old connection that pulls us together. Your body style had nothing to do with it when you agreed to meet up with them again before this lifetime. If that agreement is there, you will feel something or see something that goes way beyond the outside package.

Explaining Relationships

Sometimes it's hard to be nice when other people hurt you. We can do some pretty cruel things to each other while in relationships. You even wonder why in the world you're tangled up in a relationship with them. It's a safe bet to assume they are someone you've been with before. Whatever you two are doing that is hurtful, you've probably done that before too. The old tapes that you two share will include the hurtful things as well as the loving things you both did. When you looked at what you wanted to accomplish this lifetime, you both made this agreement that you don't remember. It said: "We will agree to meet up again. I'm going to do this to you and you're going to do this to me so we can both remember what it is we've forgotten. Then when we've had enough of it, maybe we will be ready to change it this time."

It makes sense, really. Who better to help us learn how to change things than people we have shared with before? That's why we have love at first sight. That's also why you know people who drive you absolutely crazy. You've been with them before. Have you ever met someone and felt like you've known them forever? Likewise, have you ever met someone you immediately disliked but couldn't put your finger on why? It's those very circles that pull in the ones that you need to understand that particular experience.

Let's say that you have had numerous past life experiences where several people have treated you very badly. There's a very good chance that you will indeed meet up with those people again. You are attached because you were drawn to them originally by emotions. So it's like a magnet just pulling you both together even though you don't realize you're doing it. The tendency is to repeat the same old pattern that's very familiar. Unless you understand what is going on, you will probably do the same things you have always done with that person. And the same misery or whatever you felt before will be there again. Many people get very comfortable with that misery, because they think that's all there is or it's what they deserve.

When you're in these experiences, it's part of the circle. It is not punishment. It is not something you're doing wrong. It's an opportunity for both of you. You can stop at any time and ask, "What's really going on?" But usually by the time you discover that this is not the best thing for you or you feel stuck, both of you will probably be miserable. When you are able to ask these questions, you can push the emotions aside long enough to hear what you need to learn. If you can't get to that place, then even if you get out of the relationship you'll probably run into another situation just like the last. Let's face it, if someone killed you three times, it's going to be really hard to release them. But all you have to do to change the situation is to change yourself. You don't have to deal with the other person; you just look at yourself.

Even when you're able to pick up on harmful patterns early in the relationship, you still rationalize the behaviors and emotions. You might start blaming them, but usually you end up criticizing yourself. You believe that if you just do certain things differently, things will be great. You've been working very hard to love them, and yet you can't understand why they can't love you back. If other people are wrapped up in their fear, they might not respond to your attempts to show them you care. Usually they don't feel worthy. You can't fix things for them. All you have to do is start to be aware of what you want to change in yourself. So the questions to ask yourself to get out of the situation start with, "What do I want to change about me right now?" not "What do I need to do to change him or her?"

In my work I have had many opportunities to see both sides of domestic violence. When I worked in domestic court, I was surprised to hear the major criticisms being directed to the female involved. "Why does she stay in an abusive relationship? All she has to do is leave," was what I heard most often. I never heard the question asked as to why the man had to hit.

My first case was actually a friend I worked with. Her husband worked with the local sheriff's department, which meant he had a gun. She would come to work with black marks around her neck where he would try to choke her. I tried to help her look for an apartment and even helped find some money to leave with her two young sons. The husband found out I was helping and would call my home threatening to kill me. I was very disappointed when I found out a few weeks later that she went back to him.

Upon further investigation, I found that most of these women were told repeatedly by their abusers that they didn't have the ability to be on their own. They were also often told that no other man would want them. They heard it over and over enough that their self-esteem plunged to zero. They would take up for the abuser and would accept responsibility for the abuse itself. They successfully hid it most of the time from their family and friends. Not much is accomplished until the female can see that she does have the power to leave the situation and change herself.

A huge stumbling block to initiating change is guilt. We tend to wear it like a huge boulder around our necks. Usually it's the guilt that you have intentionally hurt someone else.

Sometimes it looks like hurt when it really is you changing. People tend to resent it when they can't expect the same responses from you they've always had. Instead they will tell you that you have changed. I have had more than one client come into my office very upset because their significant other didn't like the powerful changes in them. They just assumed their partner would be elated to see them become stronger and be supportive. But most often it's the other way around. They resent the changes and are afraid. Even if they say they like the changes, their actions indicate the opposite. The resentment comes from their lack of being able to connect with you the same way and control you. So when you actually do start to make some changes in yourself, your partner might try to make you feel guilty. That boulder gets pretty heavy after a while.

Lessons

Everything I have been talking about is a learning process. When you were in the second and third grade, you didn't get the multiplication table the first time you tried it. (At least I didn't.) You had to keep on doing it until you had it memorized. At some point, in frustration, you probably said, "Why do I need this?" But the first time you had your checkbook or needed to know how to make change, you started realizing why it was so important. What if you had never learned the multiplication tables? You wouldn't be able to know if your paycheck was correct or even what change to give a cashier at a store.

This whole process is the same except it's about awareness. See it as being in school and simply reciting, which is what we are doing here, the multiplication tables. You practice it over and over, but at some point the purpose for each experience will come clear to you. The object is not to criticize or kick ourselves, but to realize that all of these lessons are part of a bigger plan that you agreed to.

How Do You Change Judging?

1) Start to be aware of some of the judgments you use daily. To do this, listen to yourself and see if you can catch yourself using words that are critical, like "good" or "bad," "punishment" or "reward."

2) Were you judging yourself or somebody else?

3) If you were judging somebody else, what was it about? What did you feel at the time?

4) What was it you were criticizing in them? Is it possible that you might have that quality too? Be honest with yourself.

5) When this happens, see yourself back at the top of the circle again. This is an opportunity to decide whether to change those qualities, keep them, or even release them. Are they really helping you?

6) If you were judging yourself—STOP. See that tape recorder inside of your head playing old tapes. Whatever it was you were saying or thinking about yourself, erase the tape. Instead, replace it with a compliment, even if you don't believe it or can't see it.

7) Try to see people, including yourself, as different packages with different wrappings. Or see yourself as an actor on a stage. Who is there with you? Why do you think you are on the stage together?

8) Give yourself plenty of time to gradually start making these changes. To help, give yourself at least one compliment a day.

You probably aren't even aware of how many times in a day you think or say something that is categorized as "bad" or "good." It's more than you think. Start to be aware of the times you are judging others and certainly yourself. Changes come in stages. You become aware of a new concept and you go out, even if it's subconsciously, and test it. You can know you are testing it when your teachers for that particular subject appear in your life. Only when you experience that test for yourself are you going to know if it is true or not.

The stumbling block is that we tend to see life through these glasses, which focus on what we don't like about ourselves. My goal in this book is to teach you how to learn to create what it is you really want. In that process you will find what it is you are looking for. But to truly understand yourself, you need to be willing to look at *all* parts of yourself. There is nothing to fear because there is no judgment on God's part—*none*.

In any part of judging, you are separating yourself. Since we are all part of creation, what you have done is slice a big gap between you and another part of God's universe. It would be like your left hand cutting off a finger on the right hand because it didn't like it. You can't really separate yourself from others no matter what you do. Instead, look and see if they are to be one of your best teachers.

CHAPTER 7

Angels

She sat nervously in front of me, fidgeting with her tissue. Her name was Carol and she desperately needed some information. She was a very attractive young woman in her early thirties. She was a professional in her field and had worked very hard to create her own successful business. She tried to hold back her emotions as tears welled up in her huge, blue eyes. She had gone to many doctors for her cancer but nothing was working. She was desperate for some help as the pain was becoming intolerable. This was her last hope. She wanted to find out information and was asking for healing with the cancer. She had often asked herself, "Why me? What did I do to deserve this?" I had agreed to try to help her as we plunged into our first session.

The introduction to her angels needed to come first. They

spent over an hour with her, talking gently and providing information to help her make sense out of the events in her life. They patiently answered her questions. They told her repeatedly that she didn't have to die. She still had time to choose other options. They shared their names and asked that she learn to talk with them directly as much as possible. Then they spent another hour working with the cancer. Only some of it was removed from the body to ease the pain. Her body had had the cancer for quite a while and to pull it all out at once would cause the body to go into shock. She ended the session with a renewed sense of peace and love.

I only saw the young woman one more time. Afterward, I didn't hear from her for several months. The doctors had been shocked to see the cancer retreat and were hopeful for a recovery or at least a remission. She was elated. Then she called about six months later and they had found more cancer in another area of her body. She was very distraught but was going to go ahead with chemotherapy. I found out through others that she had died several weeks after that.

For months I brooded over that client. I know she was repeatedly told she didn't have to die over this. So why the additional cancer? I examined everything that was done and questioned it all. Maybe I didn't do enough or should have done something different.

Late one night while I was meditating, she came to me and explained what had happened. She had already decided that she couldn't handle her life as it was. Of course she wanted to get rid of the cancer because of the excruciating pain. But she had been miserable for much of her life and finally couldn't take the misery anymore. She wanted me to know that it was such a relief to get to know her own angels. Indeed, they were right there with her when she died and she could finally see them. When she finished talking, her angels very tactfully reminded me that I really had little to do with it. They were the ones doing the talking and the work, not me. Also she always had her own choices and was a very powerful being. Just because she didn't change her mind had nothing to do with what I had done. I learned a lot from that experience.

When I get a request from someone for an individual session, they are usually at the end of their rope. They are stuck and don't know where to turn. They are also usually at a place in their life where they are ready to try something new but don't know where to go. When we have that individual session, I allow their angels to talk through me. My goal has several purposes. Most important, it is to assure them they not only have angels, but that these beings know everything there is to know about them. These angels can provide the best information that offers the person different perspectives on the various options they have in front of them. The proof of their existence comes directly from the information the person is given. Obviously it isn't information that I could be aware of. Sometimes it's even thoughts or beliefs that the person has never shared with anyone else.

I want them to realize that they have been communicating with these angels through their thoughts all along. This is proven when many people tell me after their session that they already knew what they heard. They've heard it before; they just didn't know where it was coming from. They thought it was their own thoughts. So to them it does validate that something or someone is talking to them.

I want them to feel the absolute love that comes through with these sessions. The biggest fear many people have in having a one-on-one session with their angels is that they will be judged. They not only are relieved afterward, but they feel very calm and peaceful. There never is any kind of judgment in this, never. The only feeling that comes through is pure love.

One of my main goals in life is to acquaint people with their angels. Many people I talk with hope they have some, but aren't sure. Most folks do tell me they have had situations in their life where "divine intervention" saved their life. Indeed, look at all the books out there that are testimonies to the presence of angels. We now have movies and even TV programs that are about angels or spirits. It is a good time in history to introduce humans to their own angels. Let's look at some of the most often asked questions.

Do I Have Angels?

Let me assure you everyone has his or her own angels. That means every being in the universe, living or dead, has at least one if not more angels who have been with them from the first moment of existence and through every lifetime thereafter. Believe me, they know you quite well. They are aware of every thought, word, or action you have ever had. They are as much a part of you as even your skin. They never leave your side and certainly don't disappear when you turn sixteen years old or do something you consider "bad." But before you get concerned about this, remember there is no judgment. Their main job is to simply love you so much you will learn to love yourself.

They come with you at birth and are certainly there when you die. If you choose to remain stuck on Earth after death, they still are right there with you. They do not ever leave you. Most people have at least one or two that stay forever. Others can come and go, depending on what it is you are going through. If you pray for help, there is an army of angels at your disposal. They just need to be told what it is you want or need. When you are praying in any form, they are right beside you listening and ready to help. As I said before, we are the ones who stop them from achieving what it is we are asking for. We do this by limiting the request or simply denying our ability or worth to receive it. When we use words like "I didn't think it would happen. It didn't happen this week, so it probably isn't going to. Good things never happen to me," we are literally stopping our angels in their tracks from helping us and pulling them backward.

You didn't do anything to earn these angels, so you don't have to worry about losing them. Just like the rest of the universe, they are a gift from the Creator. God felt you needed some help in this process we call life, so They created angels. These beings have never lived in a human body. They have never lived a life on Earth. They do assume or take a body once in a while to accomplish a task, but it is only for a few moments or hours. They are as perfect and knowledgeable as the Creator. They also possess abilities similar to those of the Creator, but so do you. They chose you from the beginning; they weren't assigned. One of their abilities is to see the past and the future much clearer than you can. They also remember all the things you want to accomplish in life. So they can be a great help if you let them.

They are neither male nor female, but a perfect combination of both. They don't need names because they recognize each other through different frequencies. But they do take names for you to be able to connect with them better. Often they will use names you are familiar with. They also will take a gender, again to make you more comfortable communicating or relating.

One of the angels that I use most often when talking to

groups is the archangel Michael. He is not one of my normal group of angels that I work with, but has come to help distribute much-needed information. Now some confusion has come up as various people all over the world claim to use the archangel named Michael as their source of information. Again, we are using different sources who are using similar names. It's only because those are the names most familiar to us. Gabriel is another name that is used quite often. That doesn't mean that only one person is telling the truth. Most of the information being given is very similar. It simply means that angels are using the names we expect to hear.

What Do They Do?

These angels you have all around you have various duties. First and foremost, it is to simply love you, whether you feel it or not. It's an unconditional, nonjudging love that transcends even the worst deed or thought. Second, they are there to remind you of the mission and purpose you chose to try to accomplish in this lifetime. They were with you when you reviewed your past lives and they were there when you decided what it was you wanted to do. So they remember the things you can't. One of their duties is to try to help steer you in the directions you need to go in. Third, they are here to help you with the small things and the big things you have to deal with in everyday living. This may mean advice on finances or even saving your life in an accident.

CHALLENGE:

If you find yourself in a situation where you are afraid, ask for their help. See them surrounding you, spreading their wings to protect you. If you want, you can surround yourself with a bubble of bright light. Let yourself feel the calm and joy that replaces the fear.

You usually have at least one angel whose duty it is to keep you in the body. This means they will send a feeling or thought in your head to go a different direction or avoid certain places. They can put circumstances in front of you to slow you down to avoid accidents. I had a situation once where my husband and I were late to an engagement. The faster we'd go, the worse traffic would get. I think every slow driver in the city got in front of us and around us. About a mile from our destination we saw a horrible accident that had just happened. If we had continued at our initial speed, we would have been in the middle of it. Now when slower drivers get in front of me, I try to remember that.

Many people that I have talked to share times in their life when a thought that came "out of the blue" or a "gut feeling" told them to go a different route. Later they discovered that an accident had occurred in the direction they were originally taking. Someone recently shared with me that she was driving home late at night from work. She was very tired and trying to stay awake. "Something" jerked all her senses awake and said to be careful, something was in the road ahead. It was a herd of deer. If she had hit one or more at the speed she was going, it would have totaled her car and would probably have killed her.

CHALLENGE:

Test your angels. Ask them a question that needs only a no or yes answer. Or maybe you want to just ask for their help in making a decision on something. Ask the question; the next thoughts that appear in your head are the answer. Try it for simple problems or difficult ones.

Now, you might ask, "What about the angels of those people involved in the accident?" If they were harmed or died, it was their decision. This could have been a subconscious decision, but at some level they agreed to be involved. Why would they do such a thing? We all have placed various points in our lives where, if we aren't at the place we agreed to be in life, something will happen to get our attention. Now we agreed to this before we came back this time, so you may not remember it very well. Actually you might sit and argue with me at length about your responsibility in this. But I would ask you, "If you were in an accident and are still alive, what have you learned from it?" For some it was a wake-up call to recheck their priorities. For others it was a reawakening to the beauties of the world around them. For still others it might be a decision to go an entirely different direction in their life. If you died from that accident, either it was your choice or you had reached the end as agreed upon and there was no other choice. Either way, you had the assistance of your angels in whatever decision you made at the time.

CHALLENGE:

If you are having a hard time deciding something important, ask your question right before you go to bed. They will work with you during the night and you can have your answer the next morning. You might want to write it down before you forget it. You can also talk when you are driving down the road. Turn off the radio and let everything be quiet. Ask your questions and see if you can hear them. You can drive and talk at the same time.

The other duties they perform are to help you with all parts of your life. If you are eating, dressing, working, playing, exploring, or even loving, they are there to help you. They won't ever tell you what to do. What they do is help you see all your options. You are the powerful cocreator with God. They are there to assist. Yes, they can see much clearer, but you are the one who calls the shots. You are basically in the driver's seat and they are very powerful passengers. Since there never is only one way to do something, the best way to help is to show you all your options.

If you want help with a problem at work, they are there. If you want protection for your family, they are there. If you even want financial or relationship advice, they are there. I talk to mine constantly all day. It may be asking a question or just thanking them for their presence. I even use them regularly to check up on the well-being of family members and friends. Sometimes I even ask them the best direction to take when traveling. However you choose to use them, just get used to their voice and continue a constant dialogue. If you want to protect yourself, your family, or your material things, you can simply surround the people or possessions with a bubble of light. See only light within the bubble and no dark things can enter. It works.

CHALLENGE:

Ask your angels for help when you have to do something that's difficult. If it's a job-oriented task, see it being done easily. If it's speaking to a group of people, see yourself surrounded by a host of brilliant beings. They will help you with the task, no matter what it is.

How Do We Communicate?

Let's assume you are with me up to this point and you agree you must have at least some angels around you. How do you communicate with them? They have to talk to you through your thoughts, which go on constantly in your mind. Now most of these thoughts, as I said in the first chapter, are random. Yet in the middle of this stream of thoughts come some that seem like they are "out of the blue." These are the thoughts that don't sound like your usual ones. Maybe they are telling you vital information that you need. Sometimes they are magical solutions to problems. Or maybe they are directing you to create something new. Whatever they are, they certainly aren't yours.

Have you ever been thinking about something and find yourself debating two different sides to it? This happens especially if you are trying to figure out what to do. Most people say that it's their "good" side and "bad" side that are debating. Psychology says it's the "parent" versus the "child." Often it is your angels simply conversing with you to help you explore a problem and a solution. The most common objection to this is when people tell me they are afraid that the answers they come up with are simply the ones they want to hear and not the truth. Usually they are the truth.

The angels have to talk through your thoughts because the mind is the center of creativity and your power. You would have a heart attack if some booming invisible voice came out of thin air around you. Since they have been talking to you this way from birth, it sounds like your thoughts. So the solution to hearing them is to start being aware of what is your thoughts and what is different. This doesn't happen overnight. It takes a good deal of practice.

Another way of communicating is when they come to you in your dreams. When we sleep, our conscious side tends to let go and we are more receptive to those things we cannot see. The angels will come to you as someone you trust or even a departed loved one. They take you on trips to help you solve those everyday problems. When people are in comas, they are definitely with their angels taking a long vacation. They can come back and forth, but spend most of the time with their helpers.

When these things don't seem to help or they can't get through to you, they will often speak through a coworker, a family member, a friend, or even a stranger. They will say just the right thing you needed to hear. Sometimes they will speak by pushing you toward a certain page in a book or watching a play or listening to music. The thing to remember is they are there all the time, constantly talking.

How to Talk to Your Angels

1) To start listening, get in a comfortable quiet place. Have a piece of paper and pencil in front of you. Ask a question and direct it to your angels.

2) As soon as you do this, start writing every thought that enters your mind. Don't put your pencil down. Don't even stop to check spelling. Keep writing until it feels like you have finished.

3) Does it make any sense? Usually you can tell because it won't sound like you; it will sound a little different.

4) The answer will probably be familiar because you've heard it before.

5) You can also use a computer or typewriter. Get comfortable and take some deep breaths. If you like, you can light a candle or some incense.

6) Type in your question. Then type the answer that you hear in your head, every word without stopping.

7) Look at your answers. It is them; they are just using your fingers.

Why Can't I See Them?

Most children can see angels. Maybe they can't explain that's what they're seeing, but they do see them. Sometimes they have names for their "imaginary friends." But somewhere between childhood and adulthood, we are told that they don't exist and even if they did, we couldn't possibly see them. That's why it seems so extraordinary when people do see one in human form. It's called a miracle and the person is changed. It's no miracle; it's just part of that close relationship we have.

Most people can't see them because fear or disbelief stops them. Maybe you are afraid of what you'll see. Maybe you are afraid that it would confuse you and your beliefs. Whatever it is, we are taught very early that we are to trust only what we can actually see. What's interesting is that most people differ on what they actually see. Several eyewitnesses to a crime will each have seen something different. So how can we trust our own eyes?

Which leads to the second part of the answer. You can't see them as well with your two eyes. You have to learn to see with your "third eye," which is located in the middle of the forehead between the eyes. Your regular eyes will often deceive you, but this eye won't. If you don't believe that, then ask magicians. Their work is entirely dependent upon deceiving the eyes. Everyone has this "third eye" and it is a carry-over from the earliest days on Earth, when you used it a lot. It's like looking through a camera lens that's somewhat fuzzy and can't seem to focus. If you shut your eyes, you can see through it better. Again, this takes practice.

If you don't get anything else out of this guidebook, please try at least some of these challenges. You are conversing with your angels constantly and don't even know it. Learn to listen and learn to trust their voice and help. I have seen books several inches thick that say you have to go through all these rituals to hear them. No you don't. You are hearing them now as you read this book. You can talk to them in your car, your bathtub, at work, at play, and even when you are upset. You can talk to them anywhere, anytime. It's so simple; just start realizing that you've been doing this your whole life.

CHAPTER 8

What Is Perfection?

Almost every day we hear someone around us use the word "perfect." What does it mean to you? Is it possible for a perfect evening or a perfect relationship to exist? If so, what makes it so perfect? These are difficult questions because most people have an idea of what perfect is in their head, they just have trouble verbalizing it. But if we are using it all the time, there must be some faraway place in our expectations where we reach the ultimate.

For this guidebook or the *Handbook for Perfect Beings* to help you, we probably need to reach a consensus on the definition of "perfect." To begin with, most people probably think it should only be the "absolute best" things in life or a particular experience. There would be no pain, misery, hate, or even death and everyone involved would be deliriously happy.

I was no exception to this delusion. The earliest memories of perfect expectation came at Christmas. As with most children when they are young, I would dream of the most perfect Christmas ever. I didn't realize that TV characters, magazine pictures, and friends created these expectations. I would dream that we would awake on Christmas day to find everything we ever wanted piled under a huge Christmas tree. We would then sit down later in the day to a "perfect" meal. There would be all of our favorite foods, and everyone would be dressed in their finest clothes. Other relatives and friends would join us like one big happy family. Everyone would get along and there would be no disagreements, only hugs. It was a Norman Rockwell picture in my head.

Of course every year I would be greatly disappointed. Not only could my parents not afford to give all five of us children everything that we wanted, but also Christmas dinner was not going to be pleasant. The main reason was that I was the one who had to do the dishes afterward. I was the automatic dishwasher. Mom would try to set the table with special dishes and tablecloths reserved for Christmas. But all I would be doing is counting all the dishes we were dirtying that I would have to wash.

CHALLENGE:

Take a few moments and look at what you think a perfect vacation, holiday, or event is supposed to look like. Where did your expectations come from? Was the event anything like you expected? Then think about the perfect relationship, marriage, children, and life. What would these things look like to you if they were perfect?

I have a picture of my family in our album where everyone came at Thanksgiving to our house the first year Steve and I were married. The picture is a terrific reminder of reality. I had worked for days trying to impress them with the "perfect" Thanksgiving dinner. I had carefully set out all the best "finery" that we owned in order to make the table look good. In spite of my well-intentioned efforts, the expected outcome just didn't happen. Everything seemed to fall apart all at once. General arguing had been going on all morning. We were all seated around the Thanksgiving table, except Steve, who was taking the picture. In it one of my sisters is sticking her tongue out at another sister. My brother is taunting yet another sister, who's getting pretty frustrated. Mom and Dad are very weary and it shows in their faces. Steve and I had argued just moments before the picture was taken and my body language showed it. In the middle of all this chaos is a lone little turkey that looked like it couldn't possibly make all these people happy. I can laugh at it now, but it took me a while to get over my disappointment on that holiday.

Let's look first at what perfect isn't. It isn't related to how much money you have or don't have. Now, I will be the first person to admit that the amount of money we have available to us certainly can make our lives more pleasant or miserable. It feels great to sit down and pay bills, get groceries, and maybe even have some left over to shop. If you are working several jobs just to make ends meet, you would probably disagree with me. If you are in the middle income bracket and both parents have to work, you might disagree with me. I'm not saying that it doesn't make some things easier, just that it doesn't make things perfect. I've known some pretty rich people in my life, but they didn't strike me as receptive to their life being perfect because of the money. Usually it was the opposite. They enjoyed the benefits, but worried constantly how to protect them or add more. Listen to the horror stories of people who have won large sums of money and drastically changed their lives. Somewhere we have been conditioned to believe that perfect is directly related to lots of money.

We also have been conditioned to believe that perfect means you have complete and total happiness that is the direct result of buying things. Those companies that have products to sell have to convince you that their product will bring you this total happiness. Either the people are laughing and having a great time in their new family SUV or eating hamburgers at McDonald's together. If they can convince you of this, you will most certainly buy their product. You may have to work extra hours to pay for it, but when you drive it or use it you will be happy. They know that most people are looking for something that gives them a sense of being content and peaceful. Yet, if you will watch the faces of other people around you in their cars as you are driving, not many are smiling, much less having a party. Usually everyone is in a hurry to reach their destination, very tired, or they are stressed to the limit. I do occasionally see someone going down the road with a big smile on their face. But I'm not convinced it's only related to their vehicle.

If you will watch these advertisements very carefully, you will see that they are also telling you that you owe it to the people around you, especially family, to make them happy. It's your job to keep them smiling, whatever it takes. Women are told, "If you want to please a man, then you need to use a certain deodorant, wear certain clothes, drive certain cars, and have a body like models." Men are told they have to, likewise, wear certain clothes, drive expensive cars, or wear designer cologne. Many parents believe that they owe it to their children to offer them everything they want to make it in the world. They are told they are directly responsible for creating a perfect world for their offspring. But, again, these marketing firms use guilt to convince you that if you don't give your children this certain product, their lives will be ruined. The kids sure believe it, because they are bombarded by the advertisements on their programs, as well as peer pressure to have all the "right" labels and all the "right" things available to them.

In watching cable TV with my granddaughter, I am amazed at all the advertisements aimed at her during "educational" and "fun" programs. After each one, she would emphatically announce to me that she was going to get this or that at Christmas. When we shop she wants clothes that have those TV characters on them. The pantsuits may be exactly the same as an off brand, but are four times as much. She doesn't care what they cost, she just wants that particular brand. She's only four years old and has already bought into the marketing propaganda. Of course she doesn't always get what she wants, either.

I grew up in the 1950s and '60s with the Nelson family and the Cleaver family on TV. They had to be the most perfect families I had ever seen. The parents were always loving and understanding, even when they disciplined. There were few money problems. Their home was always clean and usually calm. The mothers rarely broke a sweat when they vacuumed the house in their dresses and heels. Disasters included a "C" on a report card or getting a scratch on the knee. We swallowed every bit of it. I'm sure many children wished they had such a family. For a long time I felt I had been cheated by having the family I had. I didn't want to get rid of them; I just wanted our life to be more like the TV families.

Of course later the TV producers got smart and started showing families that had only one parent or were dysfunctional. Even though I know the Cleavers didn't really exist, I still catch myself using parts of that illusion as a guide for perfection. And it's not only me. Often through the years Steve and I have been told we were the "perfect" family. Of course the kids would snort at this and dare a visitor to hang around for a while. If they did hang around, they would find out we weren't that image they had in their head. Of course they would be disappointed and then I'd watch them continue their quest for the "perfect" family.

So we have established that having money can't give you perfection. Neither can all of those things that we work so hard to buy. You can't give perfection to someone else and neither are you responsible for their happiness. You can try to create a perfect evening or special event or holiday for others, but you can't make it perfect for them. It has to come from inside of them.

So what is perfect? It's the whole process we've been describing in this guidebook. It's the creating, the circles, the lessons, and the opposites. You can't take one part that feels good and say that alone is perfect. It won't work. As we said in Chapter 5, if you had the same things happen day after day, you would get bored. If you ate the same breakfast or dressed the same way as everyone else at the same job every day, life would be without color. It would be a monotone. If you can imagine a life with only blissful calm, peacefulness, and all the material things you needed, it would be great at first, but you would get tired of it.

I remember seeing a movie some time ago that demonstrated this. If you can overlook the violence in it, you can see what the world would probably look like if we achieved the perfect we have in our heads. It was called *Demolition Man* and it starred Sylvester Stallone and Wesley Snipes. It was placed in the year 2032 and Stallone was thawed after being frozen for thirty-five years for a crime he didn't commit. Of course everything had changed. The Earth was divided into those who lived on the surface and those who lived underground. Those on the top had achieved what we would probably call perfection. They had eliminated crime, anger, and even cursing. Everything was very peaceful and everyone seemed to have everything they wanted. Of course salt, meat, coffee, and physical sex were outlawed. Everyone just walked quietly around in togas smiling at each other.

The people who lived underground (opposites) were starving because they had no way to produce food. They were the rejects because they still wanted meat, coffee, beer, and country music. They would come to the surface occasionally and fight with the "perfect" people for food. Of course Stallone was not comfortable in the perfect world. The first thing he wanted after being thawed was a hamburger. He ended up going underground to try to catch the villain played by Snipes. Of course he catches the villain and is able to convince the people on the surface and underground to work together. The moral of the movie was that maybe perfect wasn't so great after all.

As long as we are looking at the blueprints for the universe, we should look at the blueprints for us. We are built the same way. We have to include the opposites in us and in our world in order to understand it. We, as human beings, need challenges to discover creativity and strength. We seem to need to be pushed to be motivated. Who do we honor as our heroes? Look at the history books. It's been those who were both creative and strong. They were the ones who didn't accept that it couldn't be done or was impossible. On the other hand, we use despair and turmoil to define our character. "No pain, no gain" is our motto and creed as we continue to churn out more chaos. If it doesn't cost us something, then it isn't worth very much to us. If you ask people to describe themselves, once they get past the statistics, they will often come up with characteristics that are the result of the troubles in their life.

In all parts of our life we include these opposites; we just don't realize it. Usually we choose to focus on one side or another, not both. For instance, let's say you met someone for the first time and felt yourself falling in love. The heart pounding, the feeling of floating, the tingly feelings, all these things are on one side of the circle. The other side pops up the first time you have a fight or a disagreement. You feel hurt, maybe anger, and start protecting yourself. If you had never known both the blissful feelings of falling in love as well as the painful arguments, how would you be able to understand relationships?

So it makes sense then that you have to include both opposites when describing perfect. If each balances the other, then perfect is the combination of that balance.

Actually feeling perfect is feeling centered or balanced. Notice I said, "feeling perfect," not just perfection. It's usually when someone is at a place where they feel very centered inside. They aren't being pulled or tugged one way or another. It's like having a set of scales inside you, with both sides perfectly balanced. You don't have to do anything but enjoy. Most people won't let themselves enjoy this feeling because they are craning their necks looking for the other shoe to drop.

You can feel perfect or centered even when you are very busy. Have you ever watched a leaf float down a stream or river? It just sort of bobs around as it floats smoothly in and around any obstacles in the stream. Perfect feels like that leaf that is floating down this stream. You are moving and yet everything seems to just work together. Very little effort is exerted; you just float. You still are busy and working the mind, but don't feel stressed or emotional. This is when you just let go of the things that are bothering you and hand them over to the Universe. You've done all you need to do and the Creator has to do the rest. It's interesting to watch things work out in a smooth, effortless way when you do this. It may not be the way you had imagined, but they will work out.

The opposite feels like you are stuck on a rock or stranded on the shallow side of the stream. That's when you get emotionally drained to the point you have lost your perspective. It's when you back yourself into a corner by thinking you have to get certain things done or else. It's when the people around you don't seem to be helping, but are sucking your energy and challenging your efforts. You are simply stuck and think that you have to be the one to get yourself unstuck. All you have to do is release whatever it is you are holding on to. That's all that leaf is doing. The current will pick it up when it's ready. You simply get out of the emotions, ask for some answers and help, and be prepared to go where the current takes you. It doesn't matter whether the leaf is floating or stuck; it's still perfect. It's perfect in the way it's created, the way it thinks, and the way it feels.

It's hard to recognize or even expect perfect when life is rushed and others expect so much out of you. You don't feel perfection when you are in the emotions of anger or pain. You don't feel perfect when you are trying to figure out how you are going to pay your bills or buy that car. That's OK, we don't have to feel it or even see it all the time. The important thing is to rethink what perfect is to you so you can recognize it when it is right in front of your face. Allow yourself to have perfect moments in your life. Maybe it's just a few minutes of absolute calm while noticing the brilliant red sunset. Maybe it's the warm feeling you have when you really hug somebody you love. Or it can be that feeling of exhilaration when you've accomplished a difficult task. Maybe it's that connection we can feel as human beings regardless of whether we know each other or not. Perfect comes to us in all places, all times, and all experiences.

CHALLENGE:

Take a few moments and study the sunset or sunrise. See how brilliant the colors are. Notice how it quietly spreads all over the sky and bounces off everything around it. Let the colors and peacefulness spread all over you, no matter what you are in the middle of. See yourself bathed in these colors even after the sun goes down. Give thanks for a perfect moment.

We often try to find perfection in others around us. When we hear wisdom from a teacher or read it in a book, we think the person must be very wise. We go even further to assume that these wise people don't have any problems. I know that each teacher I have had over the years has taught me a lot, but has also shown me they had things to work on too. That's a disappointing thing to find out. You expect that if they know the "truths," they can always live them. One such teacher for me was a tiny, energetic, sixty-six-year-old minister. She was the one who pushed me into hands-on healing as well as using my abilities to channel.

It's interesting that at first when you connect, you can't get enough of this person. You are so hungry for their information and energy, you don't see or hear anything but perfection in them. Then things start to happen and you gradually start to see their faults. On one hand it's quite disappointing, but on the other it's great to know they have issues and problems similar to yours. Then often you tend to invalidate them as not being who you thought they were and move on to another teacher.

This lady and I had a disagreement as to how I was going to use my abilities. She wanted them used a certain way and I didn't. Also, her personal issues would show up when she was counseling couples. Her intention was to separate the couple, not keep them together. She tried to do this to our family and it caused quite a lot of havoc for several years. We parted company and it was more than ten years before I could look back and be able to accept both sides of her. I was able to share this with her after her death three years ago. What she had to teach was true, and I was certainly ready for it. It changed my life. But she had the opposite side in her, too, and that allowed her to explore what she was here to discover for herself. I realized that I taught her a few things, too.

As I have been the teacher for some time, I know that I have disappointed many others who have gotten to know me. Yes, I am here to learn just like you. It doesn't matter how often I remind others of my shortcomings, if they aren't ready to see them yet. I have come full circle and realize that the true teacher's most important duty is simply to share information. They are not here to save anyone, but to teach people about the power in themselves. But in order to relate, they need to have similar life experiences. If I had not experienced anger, disappointment, fear, or pain, how could I understand what the opposite feels like? How could I understand balance? If teachers are to be examples, then they, too, have to have opposites. They have to know how to work with both sides for two purposes. One helps them be able to relate to others while trying to share the information they have. The other purpose allows them to create circles they want to release or change personally.

Remember, we each are here for our mission and purpose. Our mission is individual actions that help mankind as a whole or using the "good mind." Our purpose is very personal and it's what you decided to try to work on this time. Teachers have figured out or remembered some things faster, but still have others they have chosen to revisit.

The true teacher is within you. That is that voice you hear and hopefully learn to trust. It helps with everyday problems, gives you many options, and directs you down some pretty rocky paths. It doesn't matter where you go or what you get into, this inner teacher never leaves you. All the other teachers, leaders, or gurus that you come across in life are there to simply guide you to your own teacher within. Every time you hear, see, or feel something that touches you as the "truth," it provides an opportunity to awaken yet another part of your inner teacher. If you feel the need to jump from one teacher to another, take a moment and look at what you have learned from each one. I am not saying that you should stick with one teacher for forty years. I am just saying that if you find yourself moving from one guru to another constantly, you might want to see what you're afraid to change. Your true teacher within will not judge you, so there really isn't anything to be afraid of.

Remember, we are the creators of our own world. So we can create as much perfect as we can handle. You just don't sit and wait for it to happen. You decide when. How? If you can strip away the idea that it's related to your finances, the material things you have, or your attempt to please those around you, then you can start to see what it is. It's not outside you; it has to come from *inside* you. It's a frame of mind. Start with the most obvious times when things around seem calm and you feel peaceful inside. Those are perfect moments. Take them and put them to memory so you can recognize other times.

Nature is around us often to remind us of perfection. Take a few moments and look at the miracle of a flower in full bloom or explore the woods or sit by the ocean. You didn't create any of this, it's been given to you. Use these exquisite examples to remind you that if the Creator didn't overlook even the smallest details in nature, you are just as important and perfectly created.

CHALLENGE:

Try to list any possible perfect moments you might have had in the last week or month. How did they feel and what made them perfect?

I don't think that we have to be aware of being perfect all the time. If you can feel it or realize it for moments at a time, that's great. The important thing to remember that perfect does exist and is the combination of both our opposites. Use this when you are in the middle of chaos or turmoil or pain. The remembering will help you get out of emotions quicker and reach a calmer place. Then you are choosing to create a more balanced situation. You are taking control over your life. Hopefully you will be enjoying it more as you discover your own perfect moments.

Steps to Capturing Perfect

1) The next time you catch yourself being pulled into the middle of chaos, turmoil, or one of life's endless adventures—STOP. Visualize yourself as this beautiful, golden oak leaf that has fallen into a creek.

2) You are floating down the creek, sometimes very slowly and other times quickly. Whatever is in your path, you are able to easily go around it or over it. Nothing can stop you because you are light and barely touching the water.

3) You are choosing to go to the calm place inside of you. There everything is perfect, no matter what is going on outside of you.

4) When you have a difficult decision to make, don't agonize over it. Instead, tell your emotions to get out of the way. Take a piece of paper and make a scale on it.

5) On one side write the pros and on the other write the cons. Stand in the middle and see which weighs more. That's your decision. Now see the scales perfectly balanced.

6) At the end of each day, try to find a perfect moment that happened to you that day. Enjoy it again as you remember it.

7) Share something with another person for no reason. It can be a compliment, a smile, a hug, or $50. Don't expect them to behave or react a certain way. Just know that it is pure and it comes from inside you. You're sharing a perfect moment.

CHAPTER 9

All Paths Lead to the Same Place

How Is This Different from Others?

These Universal Laws differ from other theories and religions on several counts. First and foremost, they lead to the conclusion that we are each absolute perfect beings. We don't have to earn something or follow certain rules; we are already there. You don't have to hope that there is life after death. Neither do you wait and hope that you will get to the "right" place. There is no race and there is no reward. We aren't standing there holding the trophy cup at the finish line; we are the trophy cup, each of us. That means that even if you feel like you are a loser in the race of life, you aren't. You are a trophy cup, too.

Second, these laws say that you don't have to learn a whole new set of steps that will ensure you will arrive at the "best" final destination. We're each just taking different ways to get there, but we will arrive. That has to be so because everything created in the universe returns to its creator much stronger than before. So, since you are part of God's personal creation, you have to return to Them eventually much stronger than when you originally left. That's quite a promise. But even in that, God left the when and the how up to you.

These Universal Laws are already being used by each of us every day. They have been in place from the beginning and don't change or stop because you do. You are the one doing the changing. It's your vision that is changed to allow you to release, one by one, those things that hold the spirit down.

How have you been using these laws? You are creating by your thoughts every moment, whether you realize it or not. Did you have an idea about something today or yesterday? Was it a better way to do something or a solution to a problem? These are creations that you choose to act on or not. You often just don't like what you create. You are definitely creating in circles. Ask anyone if they have ever received what they asked for. Or ask most people if they have had the same things happen to them over and over. Sure they have. You are receiving the cause and effect of these circles when these events continue to reappear. What you usually do is moan and groan about being victims or being punished and send them back out, only to return to you again. So you are using cause and effect. You just don't know that it's a huge stop sign in life that says, "Here it is again and you can change it, release it, or keep it."

You can easily see the opposites of all the things around you every day. You agree that you have them, because they are labeled good or bad, young or old, and mean or kind. You haven't understood that they are to balance each other since there really is no "good" or "bad." You often talk of strengths and weaknesses or even being torn while trying to make a decision. The purpose for this balance is to help you see and experience both sides to things. So often you are defining the rose by its thorns or its petals, but not seeing the whole flower.

You seem to have the most trouble with judging. I understand that you have to explain pain and suffering some way. No one wants to admit they deserve what they get in life. Most people want to believe they are entitled to the same things as the next person if they suffer enough or work hard. You have opinions about most other people in life that rest on what little bit you hear or see. But most people work very hard to present themselves as "strong, hardworking, honest, smart, and successful." That's how they want to be seen. But what if someone else sees something different and criticizes? It hurts and you tend to want to react. When you criticize or judge someone, either aloud or to yourself, do you really feel better afterward?

This law is saying that each person is really an actor on a stage right in the middle of his or her own personal play. Unless you know everything there is to know about them, how can you judge them in any way? How can you know what is right for them? You really can't, because you don't know everything there is to know about them. Only their angels and their Creator know that information. So judging by labels or gossip or opinions isn't helping them or you. When you have opinions and say, "I wouldn't do that if I were in his or her shoes," you are creating circles that connect you to that person. You don't know what you would do in their position. It really would depend upon their script and their play. So you are using the law of judgment to hurt yourself.

You like to play with the idea of having angels. Some people agree they have them but don't know how to listen to them. You certainly ask for their help when you are in trouble or danger. You are talking to them constantly through your thoughts, but haven't learned that the other voices in your head are theirs.

The idea of perfection being who we are now, instead of after we die, is a hard one to grasp. You think you should have to work for it. You also believe that if you had it you would be rich, have everything you need, be loved by everyone, and certainly be deliriously happy. But this law is asking you to rethink what perfect is and how you achieve it. Since perfect is the creating, the circles, the lessons, and the opposites, it's already in place. You already own it right inside of you. It's very much like looking at a beautiful diamond, garnet, or topaz that's come out of the ground. There might be layers of dust and dirt on it, and, at first, it would be difficult to see the beauty of it. But once it's cleaned off, sized, and shined, it is admired for its beauty and value.

So all of these laws are the things you are already doing, thinking, or saying in your everyday life. They aren't really new. You have heard these before. "Be careful what you ask for, because you might get it." "You've made your bed, now lie in it." "Judge not that ye be not judged." These laws are being presented from a little different direction than you may have heard before. They are trying to make you aware that you and you alone have the power you need to change your life if you don't like it. All of this points back to you. You are challenged to accept all the creative ability you've received through your spiritual DNA.

Since you are supposed to be unique, this creative ability has no judgment attached to it. You each get to do it your own way. It's focusing on the perfect creation you are right now just as you read this. It gives you a chance to change what you want to change by accepting that you are creating it. You get many opportunities to do this, not just one or two. Even once you've decided to change something, you will do it slowly in steps. Since hell or judgment doesn't really exist, you can make all the "mistakes" you want, understanding they will return to you to learn from.

So the differences say that you have this unlimited power over your life. You get to make your own choices. You always have many options, not just one or two. You don't have to do certain things or adhere to a specific set of rules. You just are becoming more aware of how everything works together. The nuts and bolts of the universe are working for you to discover how connected you are to each other, nature, and God.

You might ask: "If I am already perfect, then why do I have to go through all of this? Why do I have to deal with living and dying?" If you watched the movie *Michael* with John Travolta, you know the answer to this. He plays an archangel named Michael. Now he certainly isn't the typical angel as he smokes quite heavily, drinks, and only wants to fight. But all through the movie, he keeps talking about missing the smell of the wheat field and the warmth of the sun on his face. Now angels don't really miss this because they haven't really existed in human form, but the message is there. You got so caught up in the beauty of living, all the emotions, and the sense of being a part of something much greater than yourself, that you wanted to come back each time. It's been your choice.

When I talk to spirits who are now dead, they speak of

missing certain things in their life. They miss being able to touch, the taste of great food, the crispness of the fall air. It's the pleasure, the pain, and the joy of life all rolled into one. It's interesting that you get so wrapped up in just living every day that you don't realize what you do have until you don't have it anymore. You don't miss your eyesight until something happens to it. What if you lost it tomorrow? Would you remember what the sky looks like on a summer day with white billowing clouds? Would you remember what the ocean looks like or a loved one's face? You take things for granted because you are going way too fast. We aren't taking the time to enjoy all the free stuff around us.

How Do I Know This Works?

To this I would say, "Try it. As you have read through this guidebook, what has touched you?" Whatever touched you in some way meant you were ready to change. So take just one challenge in this book and try it. See if it works for you. Again, you are already using these laws. You just aren't using them to their full potential.

I would also say, "Did you read anything in this guidebook that you already knew?" Probably so. You have heard it before. *The truth doesn't change; it just changes us.* In sharing my life experiences, I was attempting to demonstrate how all of these laws work for you in your everyday life. Even when you think you have really messed up or your life is going down the toilet, it's OK. Everything that happens to you is an opportunity to see just how creative and beautiful you are.

The bottom line to this entire guidebook is to relax and have some fun. Enjoy this trip we call life. Take time to laugh more or pamper yourself. You've been guaranteed that you are really in charge of creating your life. You've also been told that you have all the help you need from your angels and all the other powers of the universe. You've been freed from punishment, so you don't have to be quite so hard on yourself. You've been reassured that God sees you as perfect no matter what you are doing, saying, or thinking. And because of this you have it in writing that you will return to God no matter what road you decide to take.

CHALLENGE:

After you have read this book, write to me at Hampton Roads Publishing Company, Inc.; 1125 Stoney Ridge Road; Charlottesville, Virginia 22902. Share the challenges you have tried. Which ones worked for you and which ones didn't? I invite your opinions as well as suggestions. After all, we're in this thing we call life, together.

About the Author

By the time she was six years old, B.J. Wall realized that she was able to see and hear angels and the dead, but it was many years before she understood her ability.

In the intervening years she married her soul mate, an author/photographer whose work with Native Americans introduced the author to many medicine men and women who shared with her their friendships as well as their customs and beliefs.

Wall earned a master's degree in counseling in order to combine the metaphysical with the professional in her healing work. After eighteen years of providing spiritual counseling, healing, and teaching, she has recorded the truth she has heard from her angels in the *Handbook for Perfect Beings*. Its companion, the *Guidebook for Perfect Beings*, provides an intimate look at the author's experiences.

The author and her husband live near Richmond, Virginia, where they can be close to their growing family, which now includes grandchildren. She recently started the Fellowship of Perfect Beings Church and continues to teach, counsel, and write.

Hampton Roads Publishing Company

. . . for the evolving human spirit

Hampton Roads Publishing Company
publishes books on a variety of subjects including
metaphysics, health, complementary medicine,
visionary fiction, and other related topics.

For a copy of our latest catalog,
call toll-free, 800-766-8009,
or send your name and address to:

Hampton Roads Publishing Company, Inc.
1125 Stoney Ridge Road
Charlottesville, VA 22902
e-mail: hrpc@hrpub.com
www.hrpub.com